Read-Aloud Handbook

Grade **1**

Table of Contents

Introduction 4

Unit 1: Being a Good Community Member 6
Essential Question: Why do people get involved in their communities?

New School for Hopperville 8
Surfing for Change 10
Voting Day 12
The Free and the Brave: Volunteer Firefighters. 14
A Visit to the Library 16

Unit 2: Many Kinds of Characters 18
Essential Question: How do we learn about people?

Feathers Fall from Trees 20
Climb Aboard the Merry-Go-Round 22
Who Lives There? 24
Curious. 26
The Kite 28

Unit 3: Plants and Animals Grow and Change 30
Essential Question: Why do living things change?

Changes. 32
A Dad Who Has Babies. 34
Sunflower 36
Why Do Animals Play? 38
Why Opossum's Tail Is Bare 40

Unit 4: Stories Have a Narrator 42
Essential Question: How do people create stories?

Where My Aunt Rose Lives. 44
Purr Baby, Part 1 46
Purr Baby, Part 2 48
City Tug, Country Tug 50
In the Beginning of Time 52

Unit 5: Technology at Work 54
Essential Question: How can technology make a difference in our lives?

Alien Alert 56
A Special Bag. 58
Operation: Rescue Possum. 60
New Power for Vermont City! 62
Where's Taro? 64

Unit 6: Stories Teach Many Lessons 66
Essential Question: What can we learn from a mistake?

    Sticking with It.. 68

    Throwing Beans 70

    Good-Bye, Training Wheels 72

    The Man Who Never Lied... 74

    Oops! 76

Unit 7: Past, Present, and Future.. 78
Essential Question: Why is the past important?

    Pieces of the Past 80

    A Halloween History! 82

    In Grandma's Kitchen... 84

    The Glove Family, Part 1.. 86

    The Glove Family, Part 2.. 88

Unit 8: Observing the Sky 90
Essential Question: Why do the sun and moon capture our imagination?

    The Moon 92

    A Star's Story... 94

    Sun, Moon, and Wind Go Out for Dinner 96

    Man in the Moon Mystery Solved 98

    Night Hike 100

Unit 9: We Use Goods and Services 102
Essential Question: Why do people trade with each other?

    Real Jobs! Apple Farmer... 104

    No More, No Less, Part 1 106

    No More, No Less, Part 2 108

    Market Day 110

    Traders 112

Unit 10: Exploring Sound and Light 114
Essential Question: How would our lives be different without light and sound?

    Lightning 116

    Signing, Not Singing!... 118

    The Ojibwa jingle dress 120

    The Sweetest Melody 122

    Firefly Dance 124

Grade 1 Matrix... 126

Introduction

The Value of Reading Aloud to Students

Reading aloud to students is one of the best ways to engage them with the text. Students of all ages love to be read to, and as teachers read stories, poems, and informational texts to their students, they model the joy of reading and the range of genres and text types students will encounter in their own reading.

Interactive read-alouds serve the added purpose of providing teachers with opportunities to demonstrate thinking while reading a text to students. In the Benchmark Advance program, teachers are encouraged to use classic and contemporary read-alouds to model the metacognitive strategies all readers use.

Metacognitive strategies support readers to develop and deepen their comprehension of a text before, during, and after they read. Through the application of metacognitive strategies in the classroom, students think about thinking and develop as readers.

In the Benchmark Advance *Read-Aloud Handbook,* the instruction supports teachers to model and guide practice with these strategies. From grade level to grade level, as well as throughout each grade level, students review previously taught metacognitive strategies and learn how to integrate them into their reading. Through instruction and practice, students can develop the ability to draw on multiple metacognitive strategies during every reading experience.

Supporting Common Core Standards Through Read-Alouds

The read-aloud selections and instruction in this handbook support a range of Common Core Standards. Teachers support students' foundational reading skills as they model reading prose and poetry with accuracy, appropriate rate, and expression. As students listen with purpose and understanding, paraphrase the texts, and discuss ideas with peers, they enhance their speaking and listening skills. The interactive read-aloud prompts also support students' ability to use text evidence to answer a range of text-dependent questions.

Using the Read-Alouds

Within the BENCHMARK ADVANCE program, the *Read-Aloud Handbook* is listed in the Suggested Pacing Guide and in the Whole Group overview pages.

This handbook provides read-alouds for each of the 10 units in Benchmark Advance, Grade 1. You may use the read-alouds in any order you choose. Think of them as a resource to draw from to extend content knowledge beyond the selections in the Texts for Close Reading units.

Modeling the Metacognitive Strategies

As you use the *Read-Aloud Handbook,* you can guide instruction with the following model prompts.

Introduce the Passage

Read the title, share information about the author, invite students to share their ideas on what the passage is about, and engage students with additional information.

Explain the Strategy

Each unit's selections reinforce a specific metacognitive strategy. Explain to students that as you read, you will model the strategy. At least one of the interactive read-aloud prompts per selection supports the metacognitive strategy.

Read and Think Aloud

Read aloud the text with fluent expression. As you read, stop occasionally to think aloud and model the target metacognitive strategy. Use the sample prompts during reading to help you formulate think-alouds for the passages you are reading.

You may wish to write thoughts on self-stick notes and place the notes on the page as students watch. In order to keep students engaged, the *Read-Aloud Handbook* provides four think-alouds during the reading. More frequent interruptions may lead to confusion.

After Reading

You may ask questions to focus conversation on the habits of readers. For example:

• What did you see me do as I read the passage?

• What kinds of questions did you see me ask?

• What kinds of inferences did I make?

• Where did I find the important information?

• How did I summarize and synthesize information as I read? How did that help me?

• What information in the text helped me visualize?

• What did I do to "fix up" my comprehension?

Create a class Metacognitive Strategies Anchor Chart based on the information generated during your discussions in each unit. Save this anchor chart and add to it each day as you continue to focus on the same strategy.

Turn and Talk. Invite students to share examples of metacognitive strategies they used as they listened to the text. Ask partners to share their ideas with the whole group.

Connect and Transfer. Remind students that readers need to be active and engaged with the text whenever they read and that you would like them to consciously practice using this strategy until it feels natural and automatic.

Being a Good Community Member

Metacognitive Strategy: Ask Questions

Explain to students that readers ask questions while they read. Model the metacognitive strategy by asking questions before, during, and after reading the selections. Use these questions to encourage students to apply the metacognitive skill.

Ask questions before reading.	• Let's discuss the title. What do you think this selection will be about? • Let's look at the illustration. What are you curious about?
Ask questions during reading.	• What new, unfamiliar, or confusing words did you hear in this selection? • Do you have a question about a character, event, idea, or detail? • What did you find confusing?
Ask questions after reading.	• Do you still have more questions about the topic? • What is a question you had that was answered by the selection? What was the answer?

Set the Stage

Introduce the title of the selection. Identify the genre. Note how the selection fits into the theme of how people get involved in their communities.

New School for Hopperville

Engage Thinking ▸ *Do you think new schools are important to communities? Turn and tell a partner.*

Engage with the Text ▸ Read aloud the text at a fluent, expressive pace. Use the suggested prompts to model your thinking, clarify, and elicit student interaction.

1. *While reading, I wondered about the community and the school. So I asked myself a question: How many people in the community are involved with building the new school?* (Ask questions)

2. *The text says the architect drew plans for the building, so I can figure out that an architect is someone who shows how a building should be built.* (Build vocabulary)

3. *Turn and talk to a partner. Ask a question you had about how the school was built. Then have your partner answer your question. Take turns asking and answering each other questions.* (Ask questions)

Surfing for Change

Engage Thinking ▸ *Have you ever heard anyone talk about how much crime there is in an area or neighborhood? Turn and tell a partner.*

Engage with the Text ▸ Read aloud the text at a fluent, expressive pace. Use the suggested prompts to model your thinking, clarify, and elicit student interaction.

1. *I got confused about Luxolo Ponco. I asked myself a question: How did Luxolo Ponco learn about Waves for Change? Then I read that teachers or parents tell kids about the program. So Luxolo Ponco probably learned from a parent or teacher. I was able to answer my own question.* (Ask questions)

2. *Let's discuss the word* favorable. *We can use context clues to see that the empty beach made crime happen more often. So we can figure out that* favorable *means when something helps something else to happen.* (Build vocabulary)

3. *Turn and talk to a partner. Think of a question you had while listening to the selection that was answered by the selection. Share your question with your partner. Then share the details you heard that helped you answer your question.* (Ask questions)

Voting Day

Engage Thinking ► *What do you know about voting? Have your parents ever taken you with them to a voting booth? Turn and tell a partner.*

Engage with the Text ► Read aloud the text at a fluent, expressive pace. Use the suggested prompts to model your thinking, clarify, and elicit student interaction.

1. *After reading this, I have a question: At what age can most people start voting?* (Ask questions)

2. *Let's use context clues to figure out the word* privacy. *The poem talks about closing a curtain and how no one else is supposed to see the dad vote. So I think* privacy *means doing something without anyone else seeing.* (Build vocabulary)

3. *Turn and talk to a partner. Tell your partner the steps you would take to vote based on what you heard in the poem. If you become confused, ask your partner a question. Have your partner answer your question. Take turns telling each other the steps to vote.* (Ask questions)

The Free and the Brave: Volunteer Firefighters

Engage Thinking ► *What do you know about firefighters? Have you ever met a firefighter in person? Turn and tell a partner.*

Engage with the Text ► Read aloud the text at a fluent, expressive pace. Use the suggested prompts to model your thinking, clarify, and elicit student interaction.

1. *While reading, I got curious about the firefighters' test. I asked myself questions: How long is the test? Do firefighters also take a test of their strength?* (Ask questions)

2. *The article says volunteer firefighters work for free and regular firefighters get paid. So I think the word* volunteer *describes when someone chooses to works for free.* (Build vocabulary)

3. *Turn and talk to a partner. Ask your partner a question about Paul Hyman, and work together to answer the question. Then have your partner ask a question about George Washington, and work together to answer that question.* (Ask questions)

A Visit to the Library

Engage Thinking ► *Do you have a library card? What do you do when you go to the library? Turn and tell a partner.*

Engage with the Text ► Read aloud the text at a fluent, expressive pace. Use the suggested prompts to model your thinking, clarify, and elicit student interaction.

1. *While reading, I became confused about something. I asked myself this question: Is this Jesse's first trip to the library?* (Ask questions)

2. *Turn and talk to a partner. Ask each other questions about unfamiliar or confusing words in the selection (such as* aquarium, catalog, or card*). Then define these words together.* (Ask questions)

CCSS:

RL.1.1, RL.1.7, RI.1.1, RI.1.4, RI.1.7, SL.1.1, SL.1.2, L.1.4

New School for Hopperville

Hopperville needs a new school. The architect has drawn plans for a school that will have two stories, a playground, and a parking lot.

A crane with a wrecking ball knocks down this old building to make room for the new school.

Surveyors measure the ground to make sure the school is built in exactly the right place.

An excavator digs a large hole. Dump trucks take the dirt away.

When the hole is done, workers dig a trench around the edges and line it with boards. A truck pours in concrete, which is very strong when it dries. The school will be built on the concrete foundation.

Trucks bring lots of steel beams. A crane lifts them into place, and workers weld or bolt them together.

Now there's a strong steel skeleton. It will hold up the walls and floors of the building just like your bones hold you up!

A forklift carries heavy bricks to the bricklayers who are building the walls. They use a level to make sure the walls are straight.

The school looks done on the outside—but not on the inside. Electricians and plumbers put in wires and pipes.

Concrete is poured to finish the floors.

Carpenters put up walls. Painters paint.

And finally, one day, a school bus brings the children.

Surfing for Change

Kids learn to surf and stay away from crime in South Africa.

by Stephanie Santana, News-O-Matic, August 21, 2014

Big waves can be big fun. But they can also change lives! That's what Waves for Change hopes for in Cape Town, South Africa. The organization wants to help kids escape crime and get an education—by teaching them to surf!

Luxolo Ponco, age 17, is from an area of Cape Town called Khayelitsha. It can be a violent and unsafe place. But Luxolo travels to the nearby Monwabisi Beach to learn to surf. "When the gangs fight, I come here to surf and I feel safe," he told AFP.

Tim Conibear created the program to give many kids a safe haven. Before he started the program, "the beach was unused and empty," Conibear said. This "created an environment favorable to crime," he told *News-O-Matic*.

Now Conibear has helped about 250 kids learn to surf. They are as young as seven years old. Many of them did not even know how to swim when they started—even though they live very close to the beach!

Teachers or parents usually refer children to the program. They may need help with school or staying away from gangs. Now many of those kids, like Luxolo, are overcoming their troubles. And some are learning to become leaders too! A lot of the surf coaches were the program's first surfers!

Voting Day

"Is it our turn yet?" she asks her dad.
They've waited for some time.
She sees so many people
Standing in the voting line.

"Very soon," he says to her.
He squeezes her small hand.
He says, "What a special day this is
All across the land.

"It's voting day, an exciting time.
I'm glad you came with me.
Just look at all the people here,"
Her dad says happily.

The little girl looks at her dad.
She gently tugs his coat.
"Daddy," she says curiously,
"Why do people vote?"

"This is our chance to make a choice,"
He says, smiling at her.
"Voting is the way that our
Opinions can be heard.

"We get to vote on how things work
And who our leaders will be.
It's a very important part
Of living in a community.

"Every grown-up gets to vote.
It's a special gift we're given.
Our votes can change the world.
They can change the way we're living.

"All right!" he says. "It's now our turn!"
Into a voting booth they go.
She sees a special machine inside.
"That's how we vote, you know."

Her dad closes a curtain.
He says, "That's for privacy.
Your vote is just for you to know,
For no one else to see."

And now at last it's time to vote!
Her dad pushes buttons on a screen.
The votes will all be added up
By the big machine.

"I hope you will remember this,"
The dad says, leaning near.
"Our votes really make a difference.
We're making history here!"

The Free and the Brave: Volunteer Firefighters

Volunteer firefighters are important in our community. Volunteers are people who use their time to help others. Volunteer firefighters are people who help fight fires. While regular firefighters get paid, volunteer firefighters do not. Volunteer firefighters do this work for free. They do this work because they want to help.

Becoming a Firefighter

People who want to be firefighters go to special schools. They learn how to put out fires safely. They also learn how to help people who are hurt. When they are ready, they take a test. When they pass the test, they are firefighters. Both paid firefighters and volunteer firefighters have to pass this test.

All firefighters work hard to get ready for their jobs. They have to be strong. They have to carry heavy tools to fight fires. They have to climb ladders and stairs. They may also have to carry people to safety.

These brave men and women help keep us safe. They help our communities in many ways. They fight fires. They help people who are hurt. They may even rescue our pets! They may be called to help anytime—even in the middle of the night!

A Special Volunteer Firefighter

Young people can help too. They can become volunteer firefighters. They help in many ways. Paul Hyman is 17 years old. He is still in school. He is also a volunteer firefighter. He helped his fire department in a special way.

Sometimes a fire can start in a clothes dryer. This can happen if it is not cleaned the right way. Paul invented a special alarm. It warns people if the dryer is about to catch on fire. It also sprays a gas that helps put out the fire.

Paul also invented a special camera. The camera goes on a firefighter's helmet. It helps a firefighter see through smoke. This helps the firefighter find people faster.

Important Work

Not all volunteer firefighters fight fires. But they do many other important jobs. Some help a fire station run smoothly. Some may help in the office. Volunteers make sure all of the tools are working. Volunteers help clean the firehouse or the fire engines. They might go to a school to help teach children about fire safety.

Being a volunteer firefighter is hard work. But it is also a way to help others. In many towns there are not enough paid firefighters. Without volunteer firefighters there would not be enough firefighters to keep us safe.

Thankfully, people have volunteered to fight fires for a long time in U.S. history. George Washington was the first president of our country. And George Washington was a volunteer firefighter! Hopefully, people will continue to be volunteer firefighters. They help keep us safe. They watch out for our homes. Volunteer firefighters are important in our community.

A Visit to the Library

by Tori Telfer

Jesse is going to the library with his little sister Anna. Dad and baby Sam are coming, too.

"Do you think the library will have a book about fish, Dad?" says Jesse. He wants an aquarium for his birthday. "I need to know what fish like to eat."

"I'm sure they will," says Dad. "They have books about almost everything." But Jesse is still worried.

The librarian gives Jesse and Anna each a library card. Now they can check out their very own books and keep them for two weeks!

"Do you have a book about fish?" Jesse asks the librarian.

She takes Jesse to the computer station and helps him type *fish* into the online catalog. Jesse sees that the library has many fish books, but what if they are all checked out?

The librarian points toward a bookshelf that is painted blue like the ocean. What do you think Jesse will find?

The blue bookshelf is filled with fish books! Jesse even sees one called *Aquariums for Kids*. He will check it out with his new library card!

Many Kinds of Characters

Objectives
• Model visualizing

Metacognitive Strategy: Visualize

Explain to students that readers visualize while they read. Model the metacognitive strategy by visualizing before, during, and after reading the selections. Use these questions to encourage students to apply the metacognitive skill.

Visualize before reading.	• What images come to mind when you hear the title?
Visualize during reading.	• What did you imagine when you heard this? • What words helped you picture what was happening? • How did the illustration help you picture what was happening?
Visualize after reading.	• How did picturing what was happening help you understand the characters, events, and ideas? • What problems did you have picturing anything you heard in the selection?

Set the Stage

Introduce the title of the selection. Identify the genre. Note how the selection fits into the theme of learning about many kinds of characters.

Feathers Fall from Trees

Engage Thinking ▶ *How would you describe someone who works hard in order to make money to buy things he or she needs? Turn and tell a partner.*

Engage with the Text ▶ Read aloud the text at a fluent, expressive pace. Use the suggested prompts to model your thinking, clarify, and elicit student interaction.

1. *The story describes Chi and Abeo searching for feathers. I can picture bright red feathers peeking out from between leaves and grasses. This helps me understand the story.* (Visualize)

2. *The parrots are in palm trees, and the leaves are dark green. So using these context clues, I can figure out that a* frond *must be a type of leaf.* (Build vocabulary)

3. *Turn and talk to a partner. Based on details in the story, what do you know about Chi? What do you know about Abeo?*

Climb Aboard the Merry-Go-Round

Engage Thinking ▶ *Have you ever imagined yourself as someone different? Who did you imagine yourself to be? Turn and tell a partner.*

Engage with the Text ▶ Read aloud the text at a fluent, expressive pace. Use the suggested prompts to model your thinking, clarify, and elicit student interaction.

1. *The author of the poem describes the merry-go-round in many ways. I can picture the different animals going up and down in circles. (Visualize)*

2. *The poem says a circus master waves a cape. The poem also describes lots of animals. So I think a circus master must be a person who works at a circus and masters or leads the animals. (Build vocabulary)*

3. *Turn and talk to a partner. What kind of person do you think a circus master might be? Why?*

Who Lives There?

Engage Thinking ▶ *If people are wrong, do you think they should admit that they were wrong? Turn and tell a partner.*

Engage with the Text ▶ Read aloud the text at a fluent, expressive pace. Use the suggested prompts to model your thinking, clarify, and elicit student interaction.

1. *I can picture each of the animals described in the story. It helps me understand how each animal has made a different part of the house its home.* (Visualize)

2. *The poem uses the word* echoed *to tell how each animal repeated the words, "No one?" I think* echoed *means "said again" or "repeated."* (Build vocabulary)

3. *Turn and talk to a partner. How are Jason and his dad similar and different? How are the animals similar and different? What do you learn about these characters from the story?*

Curious

Engage Thinking ▶ *Do you know anyone who asks a lot of questions? Why do you think the person does this? Turn and tell a partner.*

Engage with the Text ▶ Read aloud the text at a fluent, expressive pace. Use the suggested prompts to model your thinking, clarify, and elicit student interaction.

1. *While I was reading, I imagined what the person was asking about. This helped me better understand the questions even though I cannot answer the questions.* (Visualize)

2. *The title of the poem is "Curious." Since the poem is about a person who asks lots of questions, I think* curious *describes when someone wants to know many things.* (Build vocabulary)

3. *Turn and talk to a partner. What did you learn about the speaker from reading all the questions the speaker asks? How would you describe the speaker?*

The Kite

Engage Thinking ▶ *Do you know anyone who would like to fly high in the sky? Describe this person. Turn and tell a partner.*

Engage with the Text ▶ Read aloud the text at a fluent, expressive pace. Use the suggested prompts to model your thinking, clarify, and elicit student interaction.

1. *In the story, the turtle walks to the meadow and gathers friends along the way. I can picture each animal joining the turtle as he walks along. (Visualize)*

2. *The story says that the turtle walks to the meadow to fly his kite. And the animals search through the grass in the meadow for Little Beetle. Based on these clues, I think a meadow is a grassy, open space. (Build vocabulary)*

3. *Turn and talk to a partner. At the end of the story, Little Beetle turns out to be high in the sky with the kite! What does this show about Little Beetle? How is Little Beetle similar to and different from the other animals?*

CCSS:

RL.1.1, RL.1.7, SL.1.1, SL.1.2, L.1.4

Feathers Fall from Trees

by Carol Brendler

Hollow whistles and loud squawks echoed through the misty morning air. The forest was alive with the flocks of noisy birds. Abeo covered her ears. "What are they?" she shouted to her cousin, Chi.

"Gray parrots," Chi shouted back. "They visit my village every morning. And when they fly away, feathers hide in the bushes." He pointed from the cassava plants to the oil palms. "Feathers fall from these trees."

Abeo watched the hundreds of African gray parrots perch and preen in the swaying palms. Their red tail feathers flashed against the dark green fronds.

"Today we'll be first to collect feathers," Chi said. "Then we'll visit the medicine man. He'll pay twenty *naira* for each red feather."

"Twenty *naira*!" said Abeo. "Enough to buy a box of pencils for school." She grinned. "I want to find a feather, Chi."

They waited. The sun rose higher, chasing the mist from the palms and sending the gray parrots into the cool shade of the jungle. Their whistles and squawks soon faded away.

"Now," Chi said.

Abeo felt a tingling in her fingers and toes. Soon a box of yellow pencils would be hers!

Chi showed Abeo how to look for feathers. "We have to hurry," he said. "The rest of the village will come soon, and all the feathers will be taken."

Abeo parted the cassava leaves, looking for a dash of red. Chi cried, "I found one!" He held up a sleek, red feather.

Hmm, Abeo thought. She moved closer to Chi and shook the leaves, scattering dew like rain.

"Look!" Chi pointed to a young oil palm. "Another one." He jumped up and snatched a feather clinging to a branch.

Hmm, Abeo thought. She stood on tiptoe and gazed high into the oil palms.

"Here's another!" Chi cried, pulling a red feather from the grass. He slipped it into his pocket.

Hmm, Abeo thought. She dropped to her knees and ran her hands over the wet grass. But still, Abeo couldn't find any feathers.

"Oh no," Chi said. "Here come my neighbors." One by one, people from Chi's village came. Abeo watched them stuff their pockets with feathers while they laughed and talked beneath the palms.

"Without a red feather," Abeo said to Chi, "I'll never have new, yellow pencils.

I MUST find a feather!" Wrapping her arms around a small palm nearby, Abeo rocked it as hard as she could. Palm fronds rustled overhead.

Squawk! SQUAWK!

"What's that?" Abeo squinted up into the tree.

A big, gray bird flapped its wings and flew out of the oil palm. Abeo watched it soar over the clusters of trees. Soon it became a tiny speck against the blue sky.

Something red floated down from the parrot's perch. Abeo stretched out her hand to catch it. Closing her fingers gently around her find, she called to Chi.

Abeo smiled. "In your village," she said, opening her hand to show him, "feathers really do fall from trees."

Climb Aboard the Merry-Go-Round

by Cara Brooks

Up and down, up and down,

See the spinning merry-go-round.

Climb aboard, hold on tight,

Slowly rise into the night.

Lions roar, dragons fly,

Golden coaches touch the sky.

You can be a circus master.

Wave your cape—now let's go faster!

Faster, faster, round and round,

Twirling, whirling, up and down.

Elephants and unicorns,

Shiny tusks and silver horns.

Kangaroos and crocodiles,

Bounding hops and toothy smiles.

Trotting spotted stallions race,

Prowling jungle tigers chase.

Circle, circle, once again,

Wave your magic cape and then…

Slowly, slowly, round and round,

Gently float back to the ground.

Who Lives There?

by Carolyn Matt Ford

Jason and his dad walked along a path near the woods. "Look at that old house," said Jason. "Who lives there?"

"It's empty," said his dad. "No one lives there."

"No one?" echoed the groundhog, tunneling under the sagging porch.

"No one?" echoed the spider, building a web in the corner of the basement.

"No one?" echoed the field mouse, curling up on a ragged blanket in the bedroom.

"No one?" echoed the bat before going back to sleep in the attic.

"No one?" echoed the swallow, adding straw to the nest under the roof..

"No one?" echoed the squirrel, scampering up the chimney.

"No one?" asked Jason. "I'm sure I hear something."

"You might be right," said his dad. They stopped to listen.

Jason nodded. "Yes. Someone does live there."

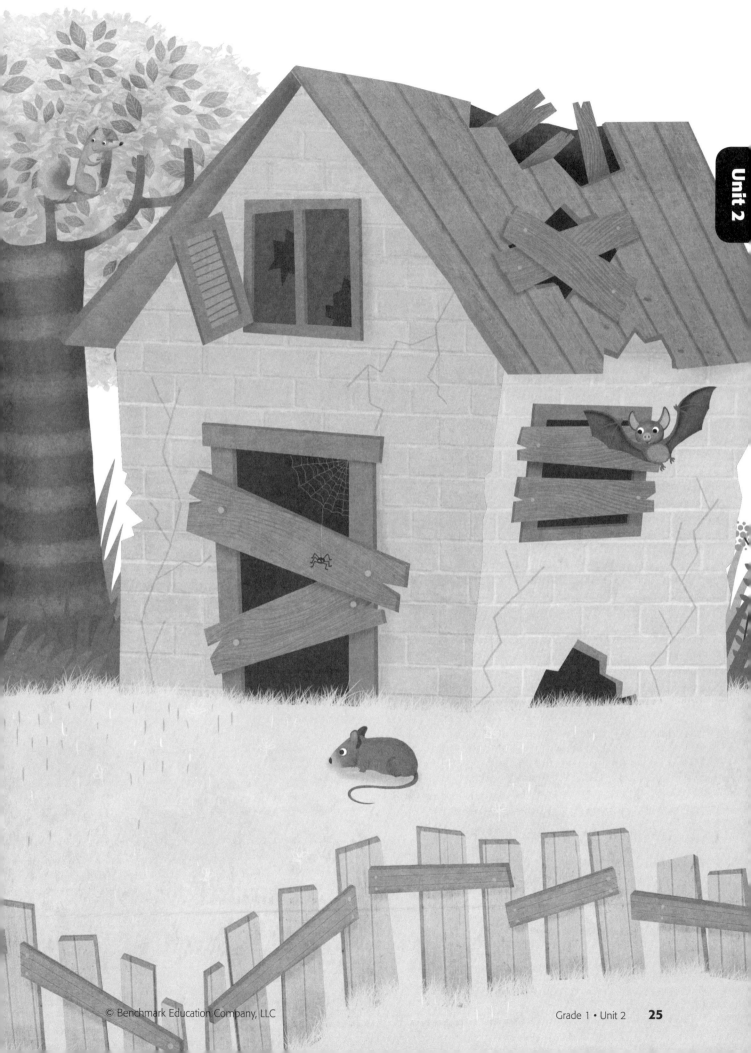

Curious

by Mary Harvey

Ever since I learned to talk,
I've just asked questions, 'round the clock.

Can airplanes fly up to the moon?
Why does July come after June?

How do Dalmatians get their spots?
Why is my ponytail in a knot?

There are so many things I wonder.
What makes the rain? How loud is thunder?

I ask these questions all the time.
Why do nickels weigh more than dimes?

Why does a bat sleep upside-down?
Why is a circle always round?

Is every tree made out of wood?
Just what is underneath that hood?

My mind is never ever lazy,
But I think I'm making people crazy!

I ask all day: What does that mean?
I ask: What makes a green bean green?

Where is this from? What does that do?
How do you make Mulligan stew?

Why is this so? How does this work?
I think I drive my friends berserk!

I wonder how a tepee's made,
And who invented lemonade.

And why my fingernails keep growing…
My questions, they just keep on going!

But I know why I ask about
So many things day in, day out.

I figured this out long ago:
It's because I really want to know!

The Kite

by Valeri Gorbachev

It was a windy day. Little Turtle was walking toward the meadow to fly his kite.

"Nice kite!" said his friend Little Mouse, nibbling an acorn.

"Let's go fly it together," said Little Turtle.

As they passed the pond, they saw their friend Little Frog.

"Nice kite!" said Little Frog. "Can I fly it with you?"

"Of course," said Little Turtle and Little Mouse. "Let's go!"

"Nice kite!" came a little voice from somewhere in the grass.

"That must be our friend Little Beetle," said Little Frog. And sure enough, it was.

"Can I fly the kite with you?" asked Little Beetle.

"Of course," said Little Turtle, Little Mouse, and Little Frog. "Let's go!"

Soon the friends reached a big meadow. They flew the kite high in the sky.

"What a wonderful kite you have," said Little Beaver, who was picking flowers in the meadow. "Look how high it's flying!"

"Thank you," said Little Turtle.

"Uh-oh," said Little Mouse.

"Where's our friend Beetle?" asked Little Frog.

The four friends looked through the grass. Little Beetle was nowhere to be found.

"Here I am!" came a little voice from high in the sky. The four friends looked up at the swooping kite. Little Beetle was the pilot!

Plants and Animals Grow and Change

Objectives
• Model determining text importance

Metacognitive Strategy: Determine Text Importance

Explain to students that readers determine text importance while they read. Model the metacognitive strategy by determining text importance before, during, and after reading the selections. Use these questions to encourage students to apply the metacognitive skill.

Determine text importance before reading.	• Based on the title and illustration, what do you think this selection will be about? What might be some big ideas or themes in this selection? • What prior knowledge do you have about these things?
Determine text importance during reading.	• What interesting text (dialogue, captions, headers, etc.) did you notice in the selection? • What do you think the author thinks, feels, or believes? • What details were most important to understanding the selection? What details did you find interesting?
Determine text importance after reading.	• What word or sentence most helped you understand what you were reading? • What do you think is a theme in the selection?

Set the Stage

Introduce the title of the selection. Identify the genre. Note how the selection fits into the theme of how plants and animals grow and change.

Changes

Engage Thinking ▶ *What is a baby animal you know about? How will it change as it grows up? Turn and tell a partner.*

Engage with the Text ▶ Read aloud the text at a fluent, expressive pace. Use the suggested prompts to model your thinking, clarify, and elicit student interaction.

1. *The title can help us figure out the most important details in a text. The title is "Changes." This helps me know that the details about changes are very important (details about how seeds, polliwogs, caterpillars, eggs, and Alice will change).* (Determine text importance)

2. *The word* polliwog *is uncommon. Based on context clues, we know that a polliwog must be the baby version of a frog.* (Build vocabulary)

3. *Turn and talk to a partner. What are some of the plants and animals in the story? How do they change as they grow up?*

A Dad Who Has Babies

Engage Thinking ▶ *What do you know about seahorses or fish in general? Where do they live and how do they grow? Turn and tell a partner.*

Engage with the Text ▶ Read aloud the text at a fluent, expressive pace. Use the suggested prompts to model your thinking, clarify, and elicit student interaction.

1. *Some details really helped me understand how baby seahorses are born. For example, the text says the mother "lays her eggs" in the father's pouch and the father carries the eggs in his pouch.* (Determine text importance)

2. *The word* pouch *is used often. The text says eggs are carried in a pouch on the father's belly. These context clues help me figure out that a pouch is a part of the father's body that is like a pocket.* (Build vocabulary)

3. *Turn and talk to a partner. What are some details you remember from the text about how baby seahorses are born, grow, and change?*

Sunflower

Engage Thinking ▶ *Have you ever grown a plant or flower? If so, how did it change as it grew? Turn and tell a partner.*

Engage with the Text ▶ Read aloud the text at a fluent, expressive pace. Use the suggested prompts to model your thinking, clarify, and elicit student interaction.

1. *A lot of details in this poem are fun, like how the sunflower is bigger than "your big brother Paul." But I don't know Paul, so this doesn't really help me understand how tall the plant is. The detail "tall as a wall" really helps me understand better. (Determine text importance)*

2. *Turn and talk to a partner. Describe how a sunflower plant starts out as a seed and grows into a full-grown plant.*

Why Do Animals Play?

Engage Thinking ▶ *Is having time to play important to growing up? How? Turn and tell a partner.*

Engage with the Text ▶ Read aloud the text at a fluent, expressive pace. Use the suggested prompts to model your thinking, clarify, and elicit student interaction.

1. *The details about how animals play to learn how to survive is important. This helps me understand a big idea in the article—that animals play in order to help them learn skills to survive in the wild. (Determine text importance)*

2. *The text says wolf pups have to learn to communicate. The text says they wiggle and move in ways to tell each other things. So I know that* communicate *means to tell each other things and understand each other. (Build vocabulary)*

3. *Turn and talk to a partner. How does playing make animals change?*

Why Opossum's Tail Is Bare

Engage Thinking ▶ *What is your favorite animal? What makes it unique and special? Turn and tell a partner.*

Engage with the Text ▶ Read aloud the text at a fluent, expressive pace. Use the suggested prompts to model your thinking, clarify, and elicit student interaction.

1. *The author includes a lot of details about opossum's tail. First, it is thick and soft, and then it becomes rough and scaly. These details help me understand how Opossum's tail changes in the story. (Determine text importance)*

2. *Turn and talk to a partner. Why does Rabbit have Cricket cut all the fur off Opossum's tail? Why do they change his tail?*

CCSS:

RL.1.1, RL.1.3, RL.1.7, RI.1.1, RI.1.2, RI.1.4, RI.1.7, SL.1.1, SL.1.2, L.1.4

Changes

by Edna Ledgard

Alice snuggled against Grandma in their favorite soft chair. Grandma opened the book. It was about changes.

On page one, Alice saw some seeds. On page two, the seeds had changed into pink and purple flowers.

On page three, Alice saw a polliwog. On page four, the polliwog had changed into a little green frog.

On page five, Alice saw a brown fuzzy caterpillar. On page six, it had changed into an orange-and-black butterfly.

Alice saw an egg that changed into a baby bird. Another egg changed into a tiny brown alligator.

"Did you ever change?" Alice asked Grandma.

Grandma smiled. "Once I was a little girl like you."

Alice hugged Grandma. "Will I change, too?" Alice asked.

"Yes, Alice. Someday you'll be a grandmother like me."

"That's good," said Alice. "But first, I'm going to change into my bathing suit and go play in the pool."

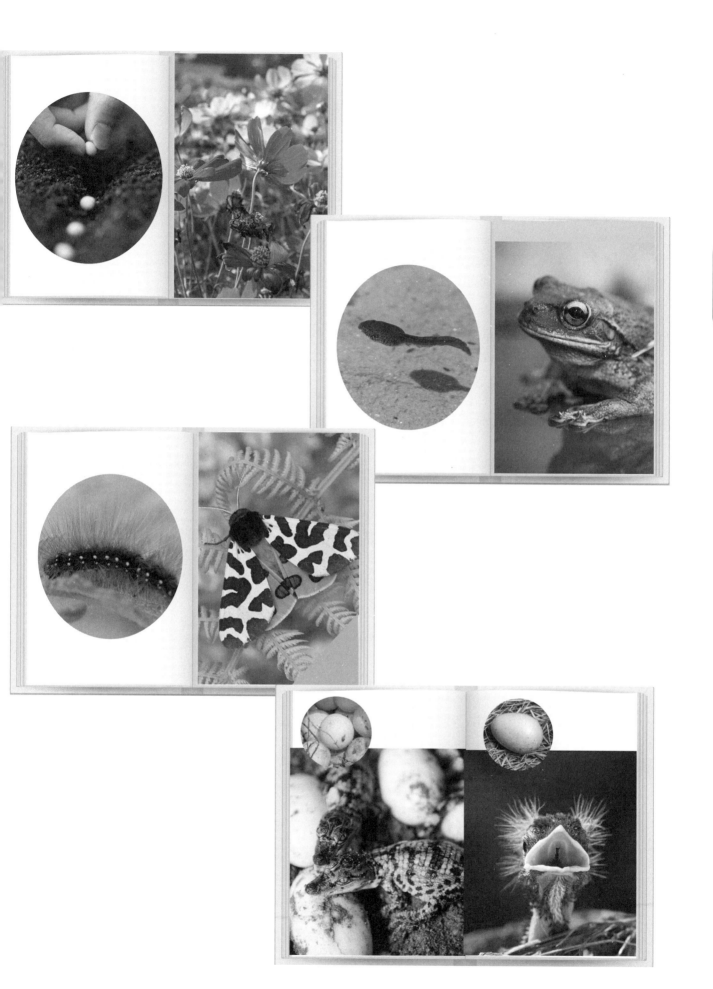

A Dad Who Has Babies

by Marilyn Singer

The seahorse lives in the sea, but it isn't a horse. It's a fish—an unusual one. Most fish swim on their bellies with their heads in front and their tails behind. But the seahorse swims upright: with its head up and its long, curvy tail down. Most fish are covered with small, shiny scales. But not the seahorse. Its bumpy, bony skeleton is covered with tough, bare skin.

Perhaps the strangest thing about seahorses is the way they have their babies. It's the father seahorse, not the mother, who gives birth. A father seahorse has a pouch on his belly. The mother seahorse lays her eggs in this pouch. Inside the pouch, the babies get food and oxygen. They grow bigger every day. The mother seahorse spends her whole life with the father seahorse. She greets the father every morning. She swims and dances in the water with him. But she does not take care of their babies at all. That's the father's job.

When the baby seahorses are ready to be born, the father grasps a seaweed stem, a piece of coral, a sponge, or another object with his tail. He bends his body back and forth. Soon his pouch opens, and out pops a baby seahorse. The tiny baby looks just like its parents. It can already swim and feed itself.

The rest of the babies are born in the next few days. They swim away and never return to their father's pouch. After all the babies are born, the father gets to rest. But very soon the mother seahorse will put more eggs in his pouch, and he'll have more babies to take care of. In just a few months these babies will be ready to be seahorse mothers and fathers themselves.

Sunflower

Whether warm out or cold,
the sunflower knows
to follow the sun
wherever it goes.
The baby sunflower plant
starts out in the tiniest pot.
It's just a little green stem.
A few leaves are all it's got!

Then the sunflower grows
and grows
and grows!

Soon you will have to place it outside.
The stalk will grow tall.
It'll grow tall as a wall.
It'll grow taller than your big brother Paul.
Once it's out of its pot
planted in a good spot
in the sun, a big green bulb
will spring out from the top.

Then the sunflower grows
and grows
and grows!

The plant will show off
petals bright and yellow.
When the summer gets hot,
the flower will be quite a huge fellow.
You'll ask yourself, "How big will it be?
Can it grow any more? No way, no, it can't.
How many seeds are growing
on my sunflower plant?"

And still the sunflower grows
and grows
and grows!

Finally, its head will hang heavy.
Its head will hang low. Full of seeds
you can gather. Seeds you can eat.
Hundreds and thousands. More seed than you'll
need!
Yum! You can eat them right there.
They're tasty to chew.
Or you can put some away.
Why not save just a few
for next year? Next year, your sunflower can
grow and grow
and grow!

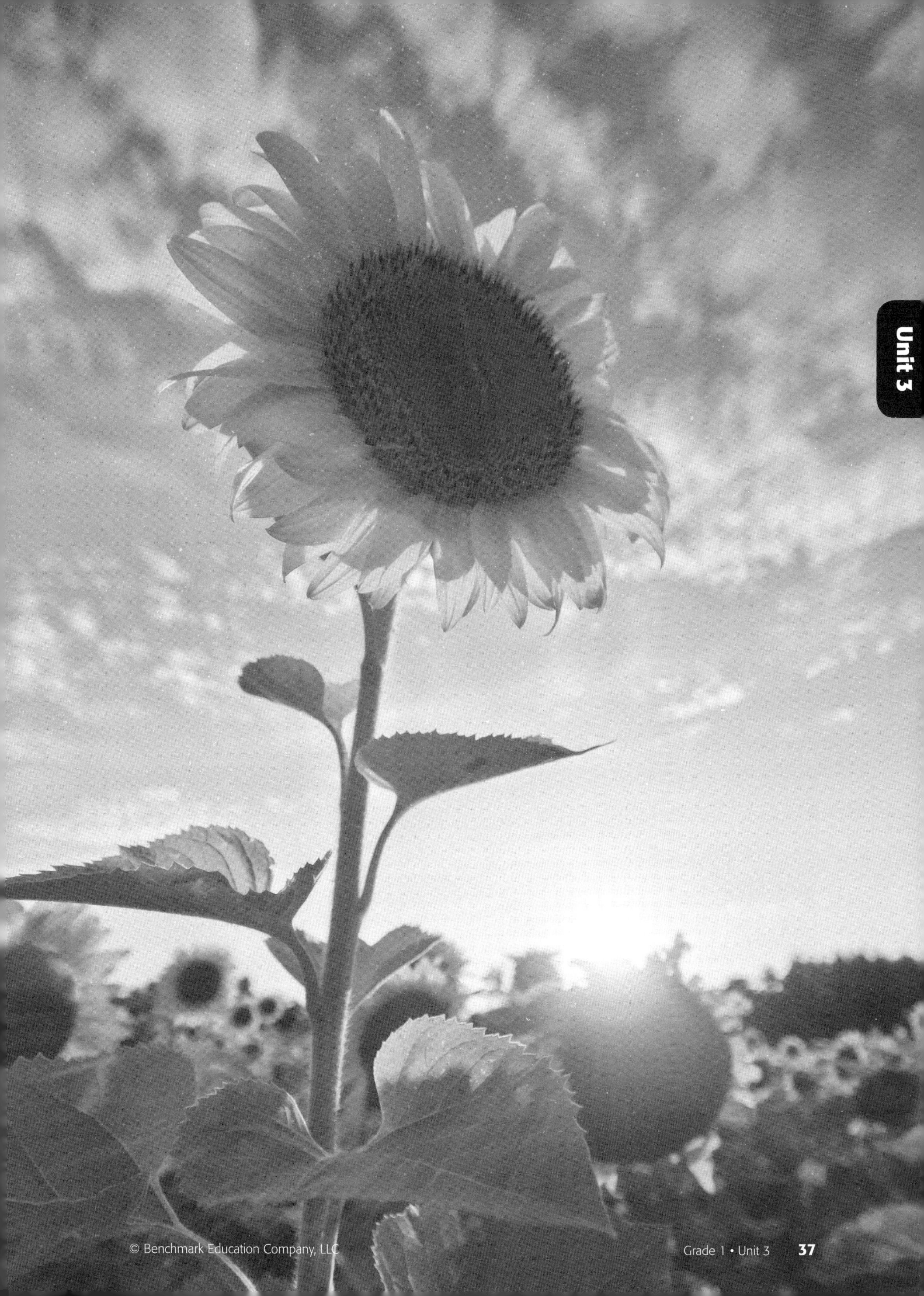

Why Do Animals Play?

by Kathleen Weidner Zoehfeld

Puppies love to run and tumble. They chase each other around the yard. They wrestle and nip each other gently. A kitten will pounce on a toy mouse or leap high for a piece of yarn.

Why do animals play? For the same reason YOU play: because it's FUN! But there is more to animal play than just fun. For animals in the wild, play is important to their very survival. Young animals have to learn about their world. They have to exercise their muscles and practice all the skills they will need to be successful adults.

Sometimes a young deer will leap and frolic. With each twisting, twirling dance, the fawn's legs are getting stronger. It is learning how to run fast and zigzag to confuse predators. That will keep it safe when it is time to leave its mother's side.

While deer have to learn to escape from predators, young lion cubs must learn how to hunt. When a cub is little, it stalks its brother or sister. It will slink along on crouched legs. When the moment seems right, the cub pounces! The other cub bats back with its paws and wriggles free.

The cubs keep their claws in, though, and their bites are gentle. The cubs are not trying to hurt each other. They are playing at being great hunters. This is practice for the real thing.

Wolves live in family groups called packs. When the pups are grown up, they will hunt together and watch out for each other. So, they must learn to communicate.

A wolf pup signals another pup that she wants to play. She stretches out her front legs and bows. She wiggles and wags her tail. As they play, both pups hold their mouths slightly open. That's how they tell each other "yes, we are still playing!"

Much like human children, young dolphins love to play with toys. Wild dolphins are very curious. They explore their world, looking for interesting items. A piece of seaweed might inspire a game. The frisky calves will chase one another, passing the seaweed from snout, to flipper, to tail.

When most young animals wrestle, race, or chase, it's not about winning. Each youngster is building its strength and skills. And they are learning to cooperate. If one youngster plays too rough, the others will let him know they are unhappy with his behavior.

Even when everyone cooperates, play can get dangerous. But animals play anyway! Young mountain goats live all their lives on steep slopes. The kids bump each other and butt heads in fun. If they're not careful, kids can fall and hurt their legs or even break their bones. When they play, the young animals learn to keep their footing no matter what might happen.

Groups of young vervet monkeys sometimes sneak away from the adults in their family. All wrapped up in their games, the little ones may not notice when danger is near. So an adult monkey will go looking for the straying youngsters. The adult will yell out a warning.

Watch out! Be careful! You've heard parents or teachers say these things when you play. Animals have to learn about the dangers in their world too. Playing helps them learn. Playing helps them get along. Playing makes them strong and confident.

Why Opossum's Tail Is Bare
(A Cherokee Legend)

Long, long ago, when Earth was still young, Opossum had a very lovely tail. His tale was long. It was covered in fur. The fur was thick and soft. Opossum felt very proud of his tail.

One night, all the animals in the forest had a dance. Opossum demanded an extra chair just for his tail! At the dance, Opossum sat down. He placed his beautiful tail on his extra chair. Whenever anyone came to speak with him, Opossum only talked about his tail. He told stories about his tail. He sang songs about his tail.

Rabbit was tired of hearing about Opossum's tail. He was tired of Opossum's foolishness. He came up with a prank to play on Opossum.

The next night there was another dance in the forest. Before the dance, Rabbit stopped by Opossum's home.

"Hello, 'Possum," said Rabbit slyly. "Will you be going to the dance tonight?" Rabbit knew Opossum would be there. He knew Opossum would want to show off his tail.

"Well, I am tired," sighed Opossum. "But I suppose I will come. I wouldn't want to let down the other animals. I know how much they love to see my beautiful tail. But I will need an extra chair!"

"Of course," said Rabbit. "Actually, I have a gift for you. Before the dance tonight, Cricket the barber will stop by. I paid Cricket to wash and trim your tail for you. That way your tail will be more beautiful than ever." Rabbit tried not to laugh.

Later that day, Cricket stopped by Opossum's home.

"You must feel so lucky," said Opossum. "I'm sure my tail is the nicest tail you've ever washed and brushed."

Cricket nodded his head in agreement. He got out a brush, a pair of scissors, and a red ribbon from his bag. He began to wash Opossum's tail. Then Cricket brushed it. Opossum sat back and relaxed. Opossum was getting sleepy.

"Feel free to take a nap, sir," said Cricket. "I don't mind. I'll continue doing my work. You can rest. When I am done combing your tail, I will wrap it in this special ribbon. That will keep your tail clean when you walk to the dance. This ribbon is a gift from Rabbit."

"Yes, you do that!" snapped Opossum. "My tail shouldn't get dirty." Then Opossum went to sleep. Cricket continued working. When Opossum woke up, Cricket was gone. It was time for the dance. Opossum looked down. He saw his tail wrapped in red ribbon. He was very pleased.

He hurried off to the dance to show everyone his amazing tail. At the dance, he sat on his chair. He placed his tail on an extra chair. Then he said very loudly, "Tonight my tail will look more beautiful than ever before. Everyone come close. Everyone look. My tail is the most beautiful of all!"

The animals gathered around. Opossum unwrapped the ribbon. But Opossum could not believe his eyes. His tail was not bushy. It was not beautiful. Rabbit started to laugh. Rabbit laughed louder and louder. Cricket laughed too. Soon all the animals were laughing.

Opossum looked down. His tail was bare! All the fur had been cut off. Now his tail looked like a lizard's tail. It was rough. It was scaly. He was so embarrassed. He fainted. He fell off his chair. He was on the floor on his back! To this day, Opossums everywhere have scaly tails. And to this day, Opossums will lie on their backs if you surprise or scare them!

Stories Have a Narrator

Metacognitive Strategy: Make Inferences and Predictions

Explain to students that readers make inferences and predictions while they read. Model the metacognitive strategy by making inferences and predictions before, during, and after reading the selections. Use these questions to encourage students to apply the metacognitive skill.

Make inferences and predictions before reading.	• Based on the title and illustration and using any prior knowledge you might have of the topic, what is an inference you can make? • Based on the title and illustration, what do you think will happen? What do you think this selection will be about?
Make inferences and predictions during reading.	• Why did the character act this way? • What do you think will happen next? Why?
Make inferences and predictions after reading.	• What do you think the character would do next? Why? • How did the characters change? How did events affect the characters?

Set the Stage

Introduce the title of the selection. Identify the genre. Note how the selection fits into the theme that stories have a narrator.

Where My Aunt Rose Lives

Engage Thinking ▶ *Based on the title, what do you think this poem will be about? Turn and tell a partner.*

Engage with the Text ▶ Read aloud the text at a fluent, expressive pace. Use the suggested prompts to model your thinking, clarify, and elicit student interaction.

1. *The poem describes people living close together. They get their sun on rooftops, and there are subways and taxis. Based on these details, I think Aunt Rose lives in a city.* (Make inferences and predictions)

2. *The poem says "vendors sell hot dogs and hats," so I think the word* vendors *means "people who sell things."* (Build vocabulary)

3. *Turn and talk to a partner. Who is the narrator or speaker of the poem? How do you think the narrator knows so much about where Aunt Rose lives?*

Purr Baby, Part 1

Engage Thinking ▶ *Do you have a story about a pet or an animal? Turn and tell a partner.*

Engage with the Text ▶ Read aloud the text at a fluent, expressive pace. Use the suggested prompts to model your thinking, clarify, and elicit student interaction.

1. *Percy hisses at Purr Baby, but Ruby feeds the kitten anyway. She seems not to care that her mother doesn't want her to keep the kitten. So I think she will keep trying to bring Purr Baby into their home.* (Make inferences and predictions)

2. *Ruby's mom says the kitten is* scraggly, *so I think this word describes how a stray cat must look, like* messy. (Build vocabulary)

3. *Turn and talk to a partner. What do you think will happen next in the story?*

Purr Baby, Part 2

Engage Thinking ▶ *Think about the story "Purr Baby." Why do you think the author decided to tell this story? Turn and tell a partner.*

Engage with the Text ▶ Read aloud the text at a fluent, expressive pace. Use the suggested prompts to model your thinking, clarify, and elicit student interaction.

1. *The mother tells the story about meeting her baby brother and how she didn't like him at first. This story cheers Ruby up–probably because it means Percy will like Purr Baby after all.* (Make inferences and predictions)

2. *If I picture what Ruby is doing when she "crouched beside Purr Baby," I know she must have gotten very low to be next to a kitten. I can use these clues to figure out that* crouched *means to get down low, or kneel.* (Build vocabulary)

3. *Turn and talk to a partner. How do you think this story would be different if it was told by Percy the cat?*

City Tug, Country Tug

Engage Thinking ▶ *Imagine you are not a person. You can be an animal, a toy, a machine, or something else. What story would you tell about your life? Turn and tell a partner.*

Engage with the Text ▶ Read aloud the text at a fluent, expressive pace. Use the suggested prompts to model your thinking, clarify, and elicit student interaction.

1. *In this poem, a tugboat is telling a story. I think the tugboat is excited to leave New York and visit new places.* (Make inferences and predictions)

2. *Based on clues in the poem, I can figure out that a lot of words refer to specific places, such as Stockholm, Brooklyn, Barnegat, Ship Bottom, Chesapeake, Susquehanna, and more.* (Build vocabulary)

3. *Turn and talk to a partner. Did the poem give you new ideas about who or what can tell a story?*

In the Beginning of Time

Engage Thinking ▶ *Around the world, people tell stories about how Earth started. Why do you think people tell these stories? Turn and tell a partner.*

Engage with the Text ▶ Read aloud the text at a fluent, expressive pace. Use the suggested prompts to model your thinking, clarify, and elicit student interaction.

1. *In this Mayan myth, two "great beings" create Earth and everything in it–but making people gives them trouble. I think the story is about what makes people different from things and animals.* (Make inferences and predictions)

2. *The word* squawked *is used along with* barked *and* howled *to describe animals' sounds, and when I say it aloud, the word sounds like a bird's cry. So I think* squawked *describes the noise a bird makes.* (Build vocabulary)

3. *Turn and talk to a partner. If you were to write this story, would you have Tepau and Gucumatz try to make people from clay, wood, or corn, or from something else? Why?*

CCSS:

RL.1.1, RL.1.4, RL.1.7, SL.1.1, SL.1.2, L.1.4

Unit 4

Where My Aunt Rose Lives

by Eileen Spinelli

Where my Aunt Rose lives,
silver subways clatter past,
noisy factory whistles blast,
dented taxis travel fast,
where my Aunt Rose lives.

Where my Aunt Rose lives,
vendors sell hot dogs and hats,
firefighters rescue cats,
grandmas chat in laundromats,
where my Aunt Rose lives.

Where my Aunt Rose lives,
people soak up rooftop sun,
splash at hydrants just for fun,
order takeout by the ton,
where my Aunt Rose lives.

Where my Aunt Rose lives,
folks go dancing half the night,
parties everywhere in sight
in the twinkling city light,
where my Aunt Rose lives.

Where my Aunt Rose lives,
neighbors finally close their eyes,
first-floor baby wakes and cries,
distant trains hum lullabies,
where my Aunt Rose lives.

FOOD

WASH N' DRY   LAUNDROMAT

Purr Baby

Part 1

by Karmen Kooyers

One morning Ruby looked out the window and said, "Mama, there's a little kitty on our steps!"

"I'm not going to look," Mama said. "We already have a cat."

Percy leaped onto the windowsill and hissed at the kitten. He arched his back and twitched his tail and knocked the plant off the windowsill.

"What's all the fuss?" Mama looked out the window at the kitten. "Scraggly and skinny," she said as she picked up the plant from the floor. "Don't bring him in the house."

"O.K., Mama. I'll just go out and pet him." Ruby found Mama's hairbrush in the bathroom and ran outside. The kitten purred and purred while Ruby brushed him.

"Are you hungry, purry kitty?" Ruby hurried back inside and grabbed a cookie from the counter and a piece of tuna loaf from the fridge. Percy paced and growled near the door.

"It's just a little kitten," Ruby said to Percy. "What's all the fuss?"

She set the cookie and tuna loaf on a fancy silver plate and carried it outside. The kitten gobbled down the food.

"Poor thing." Ruby rubbed his back, and he purred and purred.

Purr Baby followed Ruby to the backyard and played in the grass while she swung in her tire swing beside the holly bush. He waited on the steps when she went inside for lunch and was still waiting when she came out to share her cheese sandwich with him. Then he followed Ruby to the hammock under the trees. He slept on her lap while she read her books.

"Ruby Jeanne!" called Mama from the steps. "Is this my good hairbrush? And my good silver serving dish?"

"Uh-oh," said Ruby. She ran to Mama, and Purr Baby followed. Mama shooed Ruby into the house and shut the door before Purr Baby could run in, too.

"But Purr Baby's lonely," Ruby said. "And he's very hungry, too."

Mama handed Ruby some strong soap and a scrub brush. She set the silver dish and hairbrush by the kitchen sink. "Clean, clean, clean," she said.

Ruby washed the brush and silver dish. She stared out the window as the sun set in the sky, and she worried about Purr Baby. He would be scared in the dark.

"Where will Purr Baby sleep?" she asked Mama.

"Probably under the holly bush," Mama said.

Ruby shivered. "He won't like it. Why can't he sleep with me?"

Mama set Percy on the bed. "We already have a cat. Percy can sleep with you."

Percy jumped off the bed and ran out of the room. "Percy doesn't like me," Ruby said. "He's your cat. I want my own cat."

"But Percy won't be happy if we bring a new cat into the house. Did you see how he growled at the window?"

"He'll change his mind after he meets Purr Baby."

"I don't think so." Mama turned out the lights. "Now go to sleep."

(to be continued)

Unit 4

Purr Baby

Part 2

by Karmen Kooyers

Ruby thought about how scratchy the holly bush was and how the grass turned wet and cold at night. When the house grew quiet, and the stars shone bright in the sky, she tiptoed to the window. She couldn't see Purr Baby anywhere. She ran to the kitchen and opened the door.

"Purr Baby!" she called. "Purr Baby, come back!"

Mama came into the kitchen, pulling on her robe. "What's all the fuss?

"Purr Baby ran away!" Ruby cried. "I knew he wouldn't like sleeping under the bush!"

"Yes, I wondered about that, too," Mama said. "Come with me." She led Ruby to the front porch. Purr Baby lay curled on a blanket beside the wicker chair.

"Mama!" said Ruby. "Is that my good baby blanket?"

Mama laughed. "Yes, it is."

Ruby crouched beside Purr Baby and rubbed his ears. He blinked his eyes at her and purred and purred.

Mama sat on the wicker chair. "Ruby Jeanne, I remembered something tonight. Years ago, when I was your age, my mama brought my new baby brother home from the hospital. And you know what? I didn't like him. Not one bit!"

"Did you hiss and growl?" Ruby asked.

"I'm afraid I did," Mama said.

"Was that baby Uncle Bernie?"

"Yes, he was! But after I got to know my little brother, of course I loved him very much." Mama reached down and stroked Purr Baby's fur. "Maybe Percy will be glad to have a little brother, too, after he gets to know him."

"You mean I can keep Purr Baby?" Ruby jumped up and hugged Mama.

"If you love him and take care of him the way you did today."

"I will, I promise!" Ruby scooped up Purr Baby. "Come on, little baby," she said. "Come meet your new big brother."

Purr Baby yawned, and Ruby kissed his nose. "And don't worry if Percy hisses and growls," she said. "He'll love you soon enough. Just like me and Mama."

City Tug, Country Tug

by Charlotte Pomerantz

In the harbor of New York,
toot-whistle, chug-a-chug,
there are great big ships and barges,
and there's me—a little tug.

Though I'm short and sort of stout,
as anyone can see,
I can nudge or budge a barge
as large as any barge can be.

I can brave the harbor winds
which change from day to day,
as I'm scooting up the Narrows
or tooting 'round the bay.

From as far away as Stockholm,
or from Brooklyn, which is near,
ships are going in and out,
but I am always here.

Sometimes in the misty dark,
I hear a whistle blowing.
A ship is leaving old New York.
I wonder where it's going?

They say when ships are passing
by Liberty's bright light,
she often says a word or two
to guide them through the night.

To some she waves a welcome,
to some she waves good-bye.
Tonight she says, "The coast is clear.
Why not sail on by?"

And just like that, I leave New York!
Chug-chug, I'm on my way.
With a farewell toot to Liberty,
I'm out beyond the Bay!

Past Barnegat, Ship Bottom,
Great Bay, and Brigantine.
Past all the little seacoast towns
that huddle in between.

I round the Cape May lighthouse,
which shines like Liberty.
There's sure to be a harbor
for a weary tug like me.

Toot tootle toooot
Toot tootle tooooze
Tug time, snug time
to take
　　　　a little
　　　　　　snooooze—z—z—z

Wake up! It's time to chug along.
Now nothing's in my way.
Hey, look, white geese and mallard
  ducks.
Toot-toot, it's Chesapeake Bay!

Two ducks are waddling on my deck.
A goose sits on my prow
and I can see a farmhouse
with a horse and a cow.

I've never seen a farm before,
or sniffed a country breeze.
The world I've known was made of
  stone,
not farmlands, grass, or trees.

I scoot right up the Chester
And the Susquehan-i-aye,
And I toot—oh how I toot!—
at the blue crabs in the Bay.

I toot and toot again
and toot—what do I hear?
Something's tooting back at me—
a tug is chugging near!

"Where do you come from?" I ask.
"Me? From Chesapeake Bay.
It's a pleasant place to visit,
but you wouldn't want to stay."

I like to watch the true blue crabs,
their funny sideways crawl.
But once you've seen one true blue crab,
well, friend, you've seen them all."

She asks, "Where are you from?"
"Me? From New York, up the coast.
But now I'm here in Chesapeake,
the place I love the most."

Says she, "But don't you sometimes miss
the skyline of Manhattan,
the lights across the Brooklyn Bridge,
the ferryboats of Staten?"

"The only thing that I will miss
is Liberty's bright light,
which shines on New York Harbor,
all day and through the night."

She says, "I'm told New York has buildings
six stories tall.
If I lived there, I'd take my time
and try to count them all.

"I wonder what it's like," she says,
"to budge a barge up there?
Not stuck in Chesapeake Bay,
not going anywhere."

"If you really want to go," I say,
"and travel through the night,
you could be there tomorrow,
if you chug with all your might."

"Toot-toot-toot," she says, "I'm off!
Manhattan's where I'm going.
New York Harbor, that's the place
to toot and do my towing."

"Good-bye," I toot, "and when you see
the Jersey Shore, turn west.
As you pass by Liberty,
give her all my best."

Unit 4

In the Beginning of Time

(A Mayan Myth)

Long, long ago, there were no plants. There were no animals. There were no people. And there was no Earth! Everything was dark.

There were only two great beings. One of the beings was named Tepau. The other was named Gucumatz. The two were friends, and they sat together in the sky. But they were bored up there all alone. So they decided to tell each other stories.

They talked about something called Earth. And suddenly, there was Earth! They talked about mountains. And suddenly, mountains popped up on Earth. They talked about things with brown thick bases and green tops. They called them trees, and suddenly, Earth was covered in trees. They did this for many things—rocks, rivers, oceans, animals. Everything the two talked about happened. The moment they told a story, their ideas would become real.

Tepau and Gucumatz felt pleased about what they had done. But there was nobody to praise them. The mountains could not clap for them. The trees and rivers could not clap for them.

Tepau and Gucumatz commanded the animals, "Say our names! Tell us how great we are!" But the animals couldn't say their names. They couldn't clap or speak. All the animals did was make noise. The animals squawked and barked and howled.

So they decided they needed to make smarter creatures. They wanted people! People would clap and shout for them. People would sing their names in great songs.

First, they formed people out of clay. But the clay people broke apart easily. These clay people were too soft and too weak. When they broke apart, they turned into mud. Tepau and Gucumatz needed to make stronger people.

So they made people out of wood. At first, Tepau and Gucumatz were happy with the wood people. The wood people were strong. But pretty soon, Tepau and Gucumatz could tell something was wrong. The wood people knew about Tepau and Gucumatz. But they didn't care! They did not clap. They did not say "thank you." They did not sing. They did not call out their names. Pretty soon, the wood people even forgot about Tepau and Gucumatz.

Tepau and Gucumatz did not like these wooden people. So they created a large rain storm. The rain knocked over the wooden people. Pretty soon, all the wooden people were washed away.

Tepau and Gucumatz decided they would try one more time. They wanted to make the best people possible. They knew they could not use clay. They could not use wood. So they thought about it. They decided to use dough made from corn. The dough was flexible. Tepau and Gucumatz could mold the dough. They could sculpt it. They formed people and waited. Soon the people were finished. The corn people were happy on Earth. They were strong enough to care for the plants and animals on Earth. They were kind enough to feel thankful. They had minds full of creativity and ideas. They were thoughtful. The corn people sang songs about Tepau and Gucumatz. They called out their names. They thanked Tepau and Gucumatz for their lives. The corn people were exactly what Tepau and Gucumatz wanted.

Technology at Work

Metacognitive Strategy: Summarize and Synthesize

Explain to students that readers summarize and synthesize while they read. Model the metacognitive strategy by summarizing and synthesizing before, during, and after reading the selections. Use these questions to encourage students to apply the metacognitive skill.

Summarize and synthesize before reading.	• Based on the title and illustration, what might this selection be about? • Can you summarize the prior knowledge you have about this topic?
Summarize and synthesize during reading.	• What did you learn from the selection? • In general, what just happened in the story? • Let's stop reading for a moment. Can anyone summarize the details we just read?
Summarize and synthesize after reading.	• In general, what was the passage about? • What would you tell a friend this selection was mostly about?

Set the Stage

Introduce the title of the selection. Identify the genre. Note how the selection fits into the theme of technology at work.

Alien Alert

Engage Thinking ▸ *Have you ever used a computer? Have you ever used a computer mouse when working on a computer? Turn and tell a partner.*

Engage with the Text ▸ Read aloud the text at a fluent, expressive pace. Use the suggested prompts to model your thinking, clarify, and elicit student interaction.

1. *The poem is about a cat writing a letter to the government. The cat wants the government to round up all the computer mice because it likes to chase and eat real mice.* (Summarize and synthesize)

2. *The word* fossilized *is used in the second stanza. A fossil is something hard, like a rock, that was left over from years ago, like a dinosaur bone. So the cat is saying the computer mice are hard like old rocks.* (Build vocabulary)

3. *Turn and talk to a partner. How do computer mice make a difference in the life of this cat? How do computer mice make a difference in your life?*

A Special Bag

Engage Thinking ▸ *What are some types of technology that help you get to school and help you do your schoolwork? Turn and tell a partner.*

Engage with the Text ▸ Read aloud the text at a fluent, expressive pace. Use the suggested prompts to model your thinking, clarify, and elicit student interaction.

1. *The title is "A Special Bag." I can summarize what I know about bags to help me understand this passage. I know that bags are things we carry stuff in, like purses, suitcases, and book bags.* (Summarize and synthesize)

2. *The word* lamp *means "something that lights up." So we can figure out that an oil lamp is a type of lamp that burns oil. The flame produces light. That is why they can be unsafe.* (Build vocabulary)

3. *Turn and talk to a partner. What are the ways that these bags make a difference in the schoolchildren's lives?*

Operation: Rescue Possum

Engage Thinking ▶ *What are tools you use or see used in your everyday life? Turn and tell a partner.*

Engage with the Text ▶ Read aloud the text at a fluent, expressive pace. Use the suggested prompts to model your thinking, clarify, and elicit student interaction.

1. *I am going to summarize Artie and Danny's plan. They're going to build a framework and pulley system over the well with levers and rope. Also, they're going to make a harness and use bait. To me, this seems like a pretty complicated plan!* (Summarize and synthesize)

2. Levers *and pulleys* are uncommon words. They are used to describe Artie and Danny's plan. So we know these words describe types of tools or types of machines. (Build vocabulary)

3. *Turn and talk to a partner. Do you think the board Jakey used was a tool? Why or why not?*

New Power for Vermont City!

Engage Thinking ▶ *What do you know about electricity? Where does it come from? Turn and tell a partner.*

Engage with the Text ▶ Read aloud the text at a fluent, expressive pace. Use the suggested prompts to model your thinking, clarify, and elicit student interaction.

1. *This article says that most of our power comes from coal and gas, but the city of Burlington now runs on renewable energy made from river water, wind, and plants.* (Summarize and synthesize)

2. *We can use a dictionary to look up the word* renewable*. This helps us understand that the energy from the dam will never run out. So this energy will never run out and it's "Earth-friendly."* (Build vocabulary)

3. *Turn and talk to a partner. What are ways that BED's renewable energy will make a difference in the lives of the people who use it?*

Where's Taro?

Engage Thinking ▶ *Are there ways that technology can be used with our pets? If so, turn and tell a partner about it.*

Engage with the Text ▶ Read aloud the text at a fluent, expressive pace. Use the suggested prompts to model your thinking, clarify, and elicit student interaction.

1. *After Mai sees the open gate, we know that Mai's dog Taro is lost and that Mai is really worried.* (Summarize and synthesize)

2. *Sometimes authors give us definitions for unfamiliar words. The author tells us that a microchip is like a very tiny computer that contains information.* (Build vocabulary)

3. *Turn and talk to a partner. If you had a pet, would you want to attach a microchip to your pet? Why or why not?*

CCSS:

RL.1.1, RL.1.2, RL.1.3, RL.1.4, RL.1.7, RI.1.1, RI.1.2, RI.1.4, RI.1.7, SL.1.1, SL.1.2, L.1.4

Alien Alert

A Letter to City Hall, Rodent Department

by Olive Evans

I am writing to bring your attention
To a strange breed of alien mice
Lurking in schools, stores, and houses.
They are fur-less and not very nice.

Their bodies are hard, round, and oval.
Their tails are attached to a box.
When you press them, they make click-click noises
And pretend to be fossilized rocks.

These mice never squeak, run, or panic
When I stalk them or start an attack.
If I pounce on them, pat them, or push them,
They click and refuse to fight back.

What's more, they were not made for eating.
My stomach grows thinner each day.
I'm losing my fur and my patience.
Could you please round them up right away?

I look forward to sharing the future
With mice that are furry and bright.
The kind who enjoy the excitement
Of a chase through the house late at night.

Yours truly,
Thomas Cat, Esq.

City Hall
Rodent Dept.

A Special Bag

Thato Kgatlhanye lives in a town in South Africa. When she was 18 years old, she saw some problems in her town.

She saw children carrying books to school. The books were heavy. It was hard for the children to carry them. But not every child had a bag. That is because not every child could buy a bag. Thato thought every child should have a bag.

Thato saw another problem. Many children had to walk far to get to school. Sometimes they began walking before it was light out. Thato knew that walking in the dark could be dangerous. Drivers in cars might not see the children. The children might get hurt.

There was another problem. Many people did not have electricity. They used candles. Or they used oil lamps. The candles or lamps might be unsafe. Sometimes people did not have enough candles or oil. Then there was no light at night. Some children did not have enough light to do their homework.

The last problem was litter. People used plastic shopping bags. They threw them away. They did not use those bags again.

Thato decided she wanted to help. How did Thato help solve these problems? She invented a special backpack.

The backpacks are made out of used plastic bags. Workers collect the plastic bags. They clean them. Then they turn them into cloth. They sew the cloth into a backpack. The backpacks are strong. They can hold heavy books. They are also waterproof. So things inside the bags stay dry.

The backpacks are shiny. Drivers can see the shiny bags. They can see them even if it is dark out. This helps keep children safe when they walk to school.

The backpacks have one more special thing. Each one has a light. But the light does not use electricity. It does not use a battery. It uses the power of the sun! There is a solar panel in each backpack. The sun shines on the solar panel in the backpack. The panel turns the sun's rays into power. It can create enough power for the light to stay on for 12 hours!

The light helps children who do not have electricity at home. Children use the light to do their homework. They do not have to use candles or oil lamps.

Each backpack is given to a child who needs it. A school can ask Thato for the backpacks. Thato asks another person or company to pay for the backpacks. This way every child who needs one can have it for free.

Thato and her friends started a company. The company makes the backpacks. It is called Repurpose Schoolbags. *Repurpose* means to change something so that it can be used for something else. Thato and her company have changed used plastic bags into strong backpacks. They have used the sun to create electricity. Who knows what they will invent next?

Operation: Rescue Possum

by Charnan Simon

One day when Jakey went outside to play, he found a possum in the window well.

"Hello, possum," Jakey said. "You look stuck. How did you get down there, anyhow?"

The possum hissed at Jakey.

"Whoa, possum," said Jakey. He backed away. This possum didn't look cozy and friendly like the possums in his picture books.

Jakey's big brothers came around the corner of the house. "Whatcha got there, Jakey?" they said.

"A stuck possum," Jakey said.

"We've got to get that possum out!" Artie and Danny said. "Time for Operation: Rescue Possum!" They hurried to their workshop in the barn.

When Jakey followed, Artie and Danny were already hard at work drawing up plans.

"We don't want to touch the possum," Artie said. "It might bite. Besides, it looks too big to just lift."

Artie showed Jakey their plan. "First we'll build a framework over the window well. Then we'll build a pulley system on the framework."

Danny took over. "We'll need levers and pulleys and a really long rope." He made some more sketches. "If we stand almost all the way to the vegetable garden, we should have enough leverage to pull that big furball up."

Jakey looked at the plan. "How will you get the possum to stay on that platform?" he asked.

Artie and Danny looked at each other. "We'll have to make a harness," Artie decided.

"We'll clip the harness to a hook screwed into the platform, so it won't come loose," Danny said. "Then we'll lower something possums like to eat on a pole, and use it as bait to get that possum to walk right into the harness."

"Right!" said Artie. He pulled half of an old bologna sandwich from his pants pocket. "This ought to work as bait." He looked at Danny's plan. "We might need some counterweights," he said.

"Yes!" said Danny. "Counterweights are good!"

Jakey looked at Artie's bologna sandwich. It was greenish around the edges and looked disgusting. Any possum who ate that sandwich would get sick.

Jakey poked around the barn until he found a nice long board. Artie and Danny were so busy with their plans, they didn't even notice.

Jakey dragged the board around the side of the house. He slid the board into the window well. He wiggled it around until it was slanted against the corner next to the possum.

The possum didn't seem to like sharing the window well with a board. It growled at Jakey.

"Oh, pipe down," Jakey said.

Jakey climbed up into his tree house and waited. The possum sniffed the board, then poked it with one foot. Then it waddled up the board and out of the window well and into the woods behind the barn.

Jakey watched the possum disappear into the trees. Then he lay on his back and smiled up at the clouds. Operation: Rescue Crabby Possum was a success.

New Power for Vermont City!

The state's largest town begins using only Earth-friendly energy.

by Liz Lane, News-O-Matic, September 17, 2014

The United States gets most of its power from coal and gas. Now there is a city that doesn't need either! Burlington, Vermont, runs on renewable energy. Unlike coal and gas, these fuels will never run out!

Burlington Electric Department (BED) gives the town its power. It has been trying to use only renewable energy for years. BED finally met its goal this month when it bought a special river dam.

The dam collects energy created by running river water. This is called hydropower. BED also makes electricity from the wind and plants. Together, the energy sources power the whole city!

"It is exciting," said Burlington mayor Miro Weinberger. "We have achieved this … goal that helps our city make progress." Weinberger also said this new power will save money. Electricity costs will soon go down, he said.

Burlington resident Eric Pietrzak is happy about the news. He thinks the city is an example for others. "I'm proud to be in a city that is trying to pave the way," he said.

It's not just Burlington making these changes. Vermont wants most of its energy to be reusable by 2050. The U.S. government hopes the whole country will use more of this energy too.

Where's Taro?

"Taro!" called Mai. "Time for dinner!"

Usually Taro came running for his dinner. Sometimes he ran so fast he would knock Mai over. But Mai did not mind. She knew Taro did not knock her over on purpose. Taro was just a very hungry dog!

But tonight there was no sign of Taro.

"Taro!" yelled Mai. "Taro, come on!"

Mai waited. Still Taro did not come. Mai went out into the yard. Where could Taro be? She did not hear or see him. She went back inside.

"Dad," said Mai. "I can't find Taro. He isn't coming in for his dinner."

"Oh, Mai," said Dad. "I'm sure Taro is just hiding somewhere. Come on, I will help you look for him."

Mai and her Dad went outside. They began to look.

They checked all of Taro's favorite hiding places. First they looked under the bushes along the fence. Then they looked behind the garage. They even looked under the porch steps. There was no sign of Taro. But Mai saw something else.

"Uh-oh," said Mai. She looked at the gate to the yard. It was wide open. She must have forgotten to close it.

"Hmm," said Dad. "Looks like Taro got out of the yard. We will get him back."

Now Mai was really worried. Where was Taro? Was he lost? What if something had happened to him?

Dad looked at Mai. "Remember when we took Taro to the vet last week?" he said.

Mai remembered. Taro hated going to the vet. The last time they were at the vet Taro would not get out of the car. Mai had to make a line of treats from the car to the vet's office to get Taro inside.

"When we were there, the vet attached a special microchip to Taro," said Dad. "A microchip is like a very tiny computer. This microchip has special information on it. It tells who Taro's owner is. It also has our phone number. If Taro is lost, hopefully whoever finds him will take him to an animal shelter or vet. A vet can use a special machine to read the microchip. Then the vet will call us to come get Taro."

Mai thought about this.

"What if the microchip fell off of Taro?" she asked.

"That can't happen," said Dad. "The microchip is under Taro's skin. The vet did not hurt Taro when he put it there. Taro felt a little pinch, and then it was over."

"Do you think someone will call us soon?" asked Mai.

"If people have found Taro, I am sure they will call us right away," said Dad.

Just then, the phone rang. Dad answered it.

"Hello?" he said. "Yes, this is Mr. Phan."

Mai held her breath. Maybe someone had found Taro!

"We will be there right away," Mai heard Dad say. "And thank you very much!" He hung up the phone.

"Did someone find Taro?" asked Mai.

"Someone sure did!" said Dad. "Taro had made it all the way to the next town. A woman saw him and brought him to the vet's office there. The vet got our name and number from the microchip. Taro is fine. He is probably just a little scared to be in a new place. Let's go get him."

Mai was very happy to hear that Taro was safe. She grabbed Taro's leash and ran out to the car. Then she ran back to the yard.

"Where are you going?" asked Dad.

"I am going to make sure the gate is closed!" said Mai. "I don't ever want Taro to get lost again!"

Unit 5

Unit 6

Stories Teach Many Lessons

Objectives
• Model making connections

Metacognitive Strategy: Make Connections

Explain to students that readers make text-to-self, text-to-text, and text-to-world connections while they read. Model the metacognitive strategy by making connections before, during, and after reading the selections. Use these questions to encourage students to apply the metacognitive skill.

Make connections before reading.	• Let's look at the illustration. What does this picture remind you of from your own life and experiences? • This selection is a (article, story, poem). What else have you read that is a (article, story, poem)? • Based on the title, do you think this selection will tell you about something from our everyday world or something imaginary?
Make connections during reading.	• Have you ever experienced anything like what we just read about? If so, what? • Did this remind you of anything else you've read? If so, what? • Could this happen in our world today? Why or why not?
Make connections after reading.	• What thoughts, feelings, or opinions do you have about what we just read? • If you wanted to find out more about this, what else could you read? • Have you heard of anything like this in the news? If so, what?

Set the Stage

Introduce the title of the selection. Identify the genre. Note how the selection fits into the theme of how stories teach many lessons.

Sticking with It

Engage Thinking ▶ *Have you ever struggled to learn something new? Turn and tell a partner.*

Engage with the Text ▶ Read aloud the text at a fluent, expressive pace. Use the suggested prompts to model your thinking, clarify, and elicit student interaction.

1. *When reading this story, I think of things I learned from family. For example, I learned how to bake bread from my grandmother the way Fernanda is learning guitar from her grandfather.* (Make connections)

2. *The word* guitarrón *is uncommon. But there are lots of context clues: it looks like a guitar, but it was shorter and chubby. So based on this, we know that a* guitarrón *is a kind of musical instrument similar to a guitar.* (Build vocabulary)

3. *Turn and talk to a partner. What does Fernanda learn in the story?*

Throwing Beans

Engage Thinking ▶ *Was there ever a time when you were scared about something make-believe? How did you learn to stop being frightened? Turn and tell a partner.*

Engage with the Text ▶ Read aloud the text at a fluent, expressive pace. Use the suggested prompts to model your thinking, clarify, and elicit student interaction.

1. *This reminds me a little bit of Halloween. Halloween is a holiday when people get dressed up in scary costumes in order to get food. This helps me understand that the teacher in the demon costume is supposed to be fun, not scary.* (Make connections)

2. *The word* oni *is unfamiliar, but the author tells us what it means: "a ferocious beast." So we know the* oni *is the demon the teacher dresses up as.* (Build vocabulary)

3. *Turn and talk to a partner. What lesson do you think Jio learned?*

Good-Bye, Training Wheels

Engage Thinking ▸ *Have you ever felt frightened while learning something new (like how to ride a bike, ito ce skate, or to swim)? Turn and tell a partner.*

Engage with the Text ▸ Read aloud the text at a fluent, expressive pace. Use the suggested prompts to model your thinking, clarify, and elicit student interaction.

1. *This poem reminds me of "Sticking with It." In the poem, the kid is worried about learning to ride the bike before turning ten, and in the story Fernanda is frustrated as she's learning the* guitarrón. *(Make connections)*

2. *Turn and talk to a partner. What is a lesson you learned from this poem?*

The Man Who Never Lied

Engage Thinking ▸ *Have you ever been accused of telling a lie? Turn and tell a partner.*

Engage with the Text ▸ Read aloud the text at a fluent, expressive pace. Use the suggested prompts to model your thinking, clarify, and elicit student interaction.

1. *When I read about Mamad, I am reminded of a friend of mine who also always tells the truth. When the King says "no person can always tell the truth," it makes me think about our politicians. I think we have some politicians who would agree with the King and who think it's hard to always tell the truth. (Make connections)*

2. *The King says a lie can "slide off your tongue very easily." The King doesn't actually mean that lies slide. I think the King says this to suggest that sometimes it's easy to tell a lie. (Build vocabulary)*

3. *Turn and talk to a partner. Imagine the King is giving instructions to the next King. What should the new King learn about how to rule the kingdom?*

Oops!

Engage Thinking ▸ *Think about a time you made a mistake. What mistake did you make and what did you learn from it? Turn and tell a partner.*

Engage with the Text ▸ Read aloud the text at a fluent, expressive pace. Use the suggested prompts to model your thinking, clarify, and elicit student interaction.

1. *This poem reminds me of a mistake I made. I once put too much soap in a washing machine, and the bubbles overflowed. I definitely learned how much soap to put in after that! (Make connections)*

2. *The word* kazoo *is uncommon. We can look it up in the dictionary to find out that a kazoo is a musical toy. (Build vocabulary)*

3. *Turn and talk to a partner. Give your partner instructions on how to get ready for a bath. Use what you have learned from the poem.*

CCSS:

RL.1.1, RL.1.4, RL.1.7, RL.1.9, SL.1.1, SL.1.2, L.1.4

Sticking with It

My grandfather used to live in Mexico City. But a few weeks ago, he moved in with us. My mom told me he was too old to be living alone, that he needed to be with family who could take care of him. Well, I'm not sure how old he is, but he acts like he's young. He says it's music that keeps him young. He gets crinkles around his eyes when he smiles. And he smiles a lot when he's playing music for us.

When my grandfather moved in, he had only a few bags. I asked him where all of his stuff was. He said to me, "Fernanda, an old man like me doesn't need much." Then he laughed and said, "But I do need my *guitarrón*!"

I had never heard of a *guitarrón* before. Grandpa sat down on a chair and took it out of its case. It looked a lot like a guitar. But it looked different too. It was shorter. And it was chubby. And it had lots of strings. Grandpa started playing it. It had a beautiful, deep sound.

When Grandpa started playing, my mom and dad came out of the kitchen. They had been cooking a "Welcome" feast for Grandpa. Mom and Dad started to dance and swirl around the living room.

"Listen to that, Guillermo and Fernanda!" my dad said to my brother and me. "Listen to those strings—how they work together." My brother, Guillermo, rolled his eyes. But I was listening. The music was unlike anything I had heard before. I wasn't sure if I liked it. But I couldn't stop watching Grandpa's fingers as he plucked the strings. Grandpa saw me staring.

He said, "Do you hear it, Fernanda? The *guitarrón* is speaking to you."

That was a few weeks ago. And Grandpa has already started to give me lessons so I can learn to play the *guitarrón*. Now, each day after school, I go into my grandfather's room. He shows me how to hold my fingers on the stubby neck. My hands are not very strong. It's hard to make the sounds come out right. I can play for only a little while before my fingertips hurt. Grandpa says that it's important to train your hands well. I get mad, though. He laughs and chuckles at me sometimes. This makes me madder.

Yesterday I got so mad that I shouted, "Grandpa, I just can't learn how to play this thing!" Then I stomped out of his room. I stomped all the way to the living room. Guillermo was playing video games. He asked, "What's wrong, sis?"

"Ugh, I just can't play Grandpa's *guitarrón* right," I sighed. "I keep messing up the chords."

"Keep trying," he said. "It'll come."

"But it's hard," I told him.

Guillermo put down his video game controller. He looked up at me. "It took me all summer to be able to get past that one board on this game," he told me.

"So," I said.

"Well, it takes time to be able to do the things you want sometimes," he explained. "You've just got to stick with it."

I just sat there for a few minutes. I thought about what Guillermo told me. I decided he was right. So I went back to Grandpa's room. As soon as I walked in, Grandpa started smiling. His eyes got all crinkly. He was grinning. He handed me the *guitarrón*. I knew my fingers might hurt a little. I knew it might take a long time for me to learn how to play. But I decided I'd stick with it.

Throwing Beans

by Suzanne Kamata

Jio sat up straight as his kindergarten teacher called for attention.

"Today is Setsubun, the first day of spring," Mrs. Kishimoto said. "Does anyone know what that means?"

Jio slouched in his seat and buried his head in his hands. He remembered the *oni* from last year. A ferocious beast with red skin, a yellow horn growing out of its head, and fangs, it had lunged and growled. Jio had run away screaming.

All the other kids had pitched their beans, yelling, "Out with the demon! In with happiness!" But Jio had been too frightened to throw his dried soybeans at the demon to make it go away. In fact, he'd dropped them, and they'd scattered all over the ground. He didn't want to see the *oni* again.

Mrs. Kishimoto passed out squares of colored paper. "We will make boxes to hold our beans," she said. When they all had some paper, she showed them how to fold it. Jio wrote his name on his box without saying anything.

Mrs. Kishimoto put dried beans in everyone's paper boxes. Then they all went outside to the playground.

Jio looked for a place to hide. He ducked behind a tree and waited. He could hear the shrieks of the other children. The *oni* had come!

Yuki, Ayako, and Taro were running around, shouting, "Out with the *oni*! In with happiness!" Jio could hear beans pattering on the ground. Everyone sounded so excited and happy. Why weren't they afraid?

Maybe … maybe the *oni* wasn't so scary this year. Jio was bigger now. He thought he would take one little peek. Slowly, slowly, he moved his head until he could see the *oni*.

What was this? Jio saw Mrs. Kishimoto's body. On her head was a cardboard box painted red, with curly black yarn hair. A yellow horn made of a toilet paper roll was sticking out of the top, and the fangs were just paper.

When Mrs. Kishimoto saw Jio through the holes in the mask, she ran toward him.

Jio laughed. He scooped up a handful of beans and threw them at Mrs. Kishimoto in the *oni* costume. She ran away.

Jio chased her, tossing more beans. "Out with the *oni*! In with happiness!"

Soon all the beans were gone. Jio's fear was gone, too.

Good-Bye, Training Wheels

by Maggie Moran

Wibble … wobble … starting slow,
Wibble … wobble … DON'T LET GO!
Wibble … wobble … going faaaaast …
Wibble … wobble … hello, grass!

Wibble … wobble … try again.
(I hope I learn before I'm ten!)
Easy now, I'm only five …
Whoa! I almost took a dive!

Wibble … wobble … steady now,
Wibble … wobble …got it—WOW!
This is how a big kid feels.
See ya later, training wheels!

Wibble … wobble … WHOOOOA!

Unit 6

The Man Who Never Lied
(A Folktale from Africa)

Many years ago, there was a man named Mamad. Mamad was very wise. He never lied. His neighbors always said, "Oh, Mamad is such a truthful and honest person!" Pretty soon everyone in the village knew about Mamad. Pretty soon even people in other villages had heard about Mamad.

Eventually, even the King heard about this person who never told a lie. The King decided he had to meet Mamad. So he sent messengers to bring Mamad back to the royal palace. When Mamad arrived, the King looked at him closely. He didn't look so wise. He didn't look different or unusual.

"So you are Mamad," the King said. "You are well known throughout the land. Is it true that you have never told a lie? Remember, I am the King. I can tell if you are being dishonest to me, and I can have you punished!" The King frowned down at Mamad.

"My King," said Mamad, "what you heard is true."

"Hmmph," said the King. "But can you promise that you will never tell a lie for the rest of your life?"

"Yes," said Mamad. "I will never lie."

"Well, that is a big promise," said the King. "But you better be careful, Mamad. For a lie is very crafty. A lie is very tricky. Before you know it, a lie can slide off your tongue very easily." The King thought more about Mamad. He was worried people would think Mamad was wiser than he was. So he came up with a plan.

"Mamad," said the King, "I must end our chat now for I plan to go hunting. Come, walk with me out of the castle." Outside the castle, a crowd had formed. Everyone wanted to see Mamad with the King. The King held the rein of his horse. He put his foot into the stirrup of his saddle.

"Mamad," commanded the King, "go to the summer palace. There, you will find the Queen. Go now. Go quickly. Tell the Queen I will be there for lunch."

Mamad agreed. As soon as Mamad was gone, the King began to laugh.

He said to the crowd, "I never planned to go hunting. All this was to catch Mamad in a lie. Now Mamad will lie to the Queen. No person can always tell the truth. This will prove it."

When Mamad arrived at the summer palace, he found the Queen. But instead of giving her the King's message, he said "The King might be here for lunch. Or he might not. So maybe you will need to have a big feast ready. Or maybe not."

"Might? Maybe? Mamad, just tell me. Will the King be here for lunch or not?" the Queen demanded.

"I don't know," explained Mamad. "I saw him put one foot in the stirrup. But I don't know if he put his other foot in the stirrup after I left. He might have, or he might have put his foot back on the ground."

Late in the evening, the King finally arrived.

"Supposedly Mamad never tells a lie," said the King. "But I know for a fact that he lied to you today!" The King smiled, pleased with himself.

The Queen then told the King exactly what Mamad said. The King realized that a wise person never lies and always tells the truth. And that wise people only say what they have seen with their own eyes. The King realized, then, how wrong it was to have tried to set Mamad up to lie. He decided, from then on, to rule his kingdom with truth and honesty.

Oops!

I turned on the water
to fill up my tub.
Time to jump in those bubbles
and scrub, scrub, scrub.

As I waited, I picked up
a new pop-up book.
I was just going to take
a very short look.

Then some playing cards
caught my eye.
There was a magic trick
I just had to try.

Then I wanted to walk in
my grandmother's shoes,
and I needed a minute
to play my kazoo.

Then I needed to finish
a painting I'd started
of a slimy, green dragon
and a castle it guarded.

But all that time, I'd forgotten.
Oh, gee! And oh no!
By then, my bath water
had all overflowed!

What a mess I had made!
What a terrible scene.
My parents were angry.
It took me a long time to clean!

So to you, my dear friends,
I would just like to mention:
If the water is running,
please do pay attention!

Objectives
• Model using fix-up monitoring strategies

Metacognitive Strategy: Use Fix-up monitoring Strategies

Explain to students that readers self-monitor to fix comprehension while they read. Model the metacognitive strategy by self-monitoring to fix comprehension before, during, and after reading the selections. Use these questions to encourage students to apply the metacognitive skill.

Use fix-up monitoring strategies before reading.	• Let's read the title. What do you find confusing about this topic? • Let's look at the illustration. What do you find confusing in the illustration?
Use fix-up monitoring strategies during reading.	• Let's stop. Can you explain what just happened? • What is a detail that confused you? Let's read ahead to try to figure it out.
Use fix-up monitoring strategies after reading.	• Did any part of the story confuse you? If so, let's reread that part of the story. • Talk to a partner about something in the selection that confused you.

Set the Stage

Introduce the title of the selection. Identify the genre. Note how the selection fits into the theme of the past, present, and future.

Pieces of the Past

Engage Thinking ▸ *If you could send a message to people in the future, what would you tell them? Turn and tell a partner.*

Engage with the Text ▸ Read aloud the text at a fluent, expressive pace. Use the suggested prompts to model your thinking, clarify, and elicit student interaction.

1. *I got confused after reading the second paragraph. I didn't know what a time capsule is. So I decided to read ahead, and I found out what a time capsule is in the third paragraph.* (Use fix-up monitoring strategies)

2. *I think I know the word* earphones, *but I can make sure by checking a dictionary. Now I know that* earphones *are tiny things that fit in or on your ears and produce sound, like music.* (Build vocabulary)

3. *Turn and talk to a partner. Do you think it was interesting for people in 2014 to open the time capsule from 1914? Why or why not?*

A Halloween History!

Engage Thinking ▸ *How do people celebrate Halloween nowadays? Do you know how people celebrated in the past? Turn and tell a partner.*

Engage with the Text ▸ Read aloud the text at a fluent, expressive pace. Use the suggested prompts to model your thinking, clarify, and elicit student interaction.

1. *I got confused in the second paragraph, so I reread to better understand. We celebrate New Year on January 1, but in the past the ancient Celts celebrated it on a different day (November 1), which means that October 31 was like their New Year's Eve.* (Use fix-up monitoring strategies)

2. *Turn and talk to a partner. Based on this article, do you think traditions from the past are important? Why or why not?*

In Grandma's Kitchen

Engage Thinking ▶ *Think about your family's history. Has your family always lived in the same place? Have you moved? Do you have relatives from other countries? Turn and tell a partner.*

Engage with the Text ▶ Read aloud the text at a fluent, expressive pace. Use the suggested prompts to model your thinking, clarify, and elicit student interaction.

1. *I got confused when the speaker's grandma says "My mother taught me this." After rereading, I realized that the speaker's great-grandma taught the grandma how to cook. Now I understand.* (Use fix-up monitoring strategies)

2. *The poem says the great-grandma was from Italy originally. We can use these clues to figure out that originally means first. So Italy is where she first lived.* (Build vocabulary)

3. *Turn and talk to a partner. Do you think it is important that the grandma is teaching the speaker how to cook spaghetti sauce and meatballs? Why or why not?*

The Glove Family, Part 1

Engage Thinking ▶ *Have older family members or friends told you stories about when they were young? Turn and tell a partner.*

Engage with the Text ▶ Read aloud the text at a fluent, expressive pace. Use the suggested prompts to model your thinking, clarify, and elicit student interaction.

1. *I got confused in the fourth paragraph. So I asked myself a question, "How could tea help Mommika's fingers?" Then I thought about cups of tea. They're warm. So I think the warmth was supposed to help Mommika's fingers but did not.* (Use fix-up monitoring strategies)

2. *The word x-rays is uncommon. The story says the doctor took x-rays of Mommika's hands. So we can figure out that x-rays must be a way doctors can find out more information about a person's body.* (Build vocabulary)

3. *Turn and talk to a partner. Do you think it is important that Mommika tell Annuska stories about the past? Why or why not?*

The Glove Family, Part 2

Engage Thinking ▶ *What did you learn about Mommika's past from the first part of "The Glove Family" story? Turn and tell a partner.*

Engage with the Text ▶ Read aloud the text at a fluent, expressive pace. Use the suggested prompts to model your thinking, clarify, and elicit student interaction.

1. *I got confused when I couldn't recall who Peti is. So I skimmed the first half of the story. I found out that Peti was the youngest of Mommika's nine brothers and sisters.* (Use fix-up monitoring strategies)

2. *Annuska embroiders the gloves. The story says she is using thread and makes tiny faces, braids, and hair. So these clues tell us that the meaning of embroider is "to stitch small details with thread."* (Build vocabulary)

3. *Turn and talk to a partner. How does Annuska's ability to sew show that she is carrying on a family tradition from the past?*

CCSS:

RL.1.1, RL.1.4, RL.1.7, RI.1.1, RI.1.2, RI.1.4, RI.1.7, SL.1.2, L.1.4

Unit 7

Pieces of the Past

Pretend you are writing a letter to people in the future. These are people who live a long time in the future. Years and years! What kinds of things would you want to tell them? Will you tell them about the food you eat? Or the books you read? Maybe you will tell them about the music you like to listen to. Or the clothes you wear.

Or you could give these things to people in the future. How can you do this? By making a time capsule.

A time capsule is a special container. To make a time capsule, people choose things that show what life is like for them. Then they put these things in a container. The container could be an empty coffee tin. Or it could be a plastic or metal box. The box is locked up tight. Then it is put away in a safe place. Sometimes it is buried underground. After some time has passed, the box can be opened.

Time capsules can hold many different things. In 1938 people in New York created a time capsule. People put many things inside it. There was a toothbrush, a baseball, toy blocks, seeds, a dictionary, and photographs. There was also a letter to the people who will open the time capsule in the future. Then the time capsule was buried deep underground. It will stay buried for 5,000 years! Can you imagine who might find it?

Sometimes people forget about their time capsules. In 1914 some people made a time capsule. They wanted it to stay closed for 60 years. They wanted it to be opened in 1974. But the time capsule was lost. No one knew where it was! It could not be found. So it could not be opened.

Finally, the time capsule was found. It was opened in 2014. There were many interesting papers inside it. They told what life was like in 1914. The people who opened it wanted to put more things in it. Then they wanted to close it again. Some children picked things to put in the time capsule. They wanted to show things from life today. They put in earphones and books. They put in a subway pass and even paper coffee cups! This time capsule will be opened again in 100 years.

Not all time capsules have to be buried underground. You do not even have to wait a long time to open them! You can make your own time capsule. Here is how:

Find a box or other container. Make sure it will last for a while. Write your name and the date on it. Then write when you want it to be opened. You can even decorate it.

Find a place to keep your time capsule. Make sure the place is dry so the time capsule will not get wet. Make sure your time capsule will fit in the space.

Choose some things that show who you are. They can be anything you want. Just make sure they will fit inside your time capsule! You might choose toys or your favorite book. You can also add photos. You might even add a recipe for one of your favorite foods.

Write a letter. Address it to whoever will find your time capsule. You could write the letter to a stranger. Or you could write the letter to yourself! Tell who you are. Tell what you like to do. Maybe even tell things you think might happen in the future. Who knows? You might be right!

Unit 7

A Halloween History!

Learn how Halloween started in America!

by Russell Kahn, News-O-Matic, October 24, 2014

Trick or treat! For most kids, Halloween is a day of candy. But where did it come from? Most people think it started from the Celts (KELTS). That was a group of people in Europe thousands of years ago.

The ancient Celts celebrated their new year on November 1. The day was called All Souls' Day. They believed ghosts would come out the day before, October 31! That night, Celts had a festival called Samhain. They wore costumes to hide from the ghosts.

Irish people brought this tradition to the United States. They also brought the art of making jack-o'-lanterns. The name "Jack" comes from the Irish story of Stingy Jack. A light inside a pumpkin kept his ghost away.

Some also think the Irish brought the custom of playing harmless tricks. People sometimes gave treats to stop the tricks. By the 1920s, kids started saying, "Trick or treat!"

Halloween soon became a big, spooky holiday! Wherever you are, have a happy Halloween!

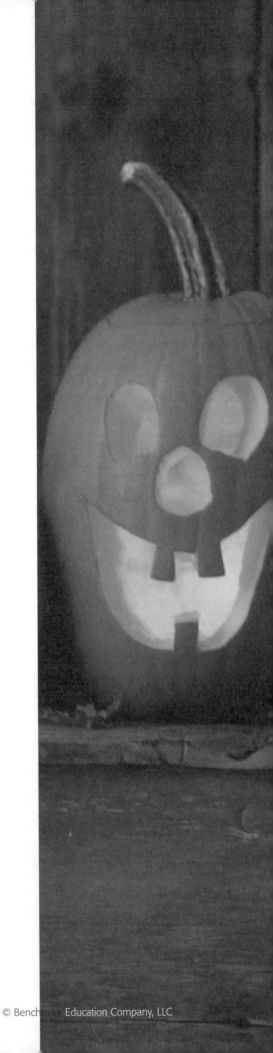

In Grandma's Kitchen

Onions, spices, garlic cloves,
The smells are tickling my nose.

Tomatoes, olive oil too—
Grandma shows me what to do.

We chop and cut. We get things ready.
We're making sauce for our spaghetti!

In Grandma's pot, we stir and stir.
Oh how I love to cook with her!

"My mother taught me this, you know,"
Says Grandma as her smile grows.

"She learned to cook in Italy
Where she was from originally."

In a big round bowl, we mix ground meat.
We're making meatballs—what a treat!

We add a slice of moistened bread,
Parsley, pepper, salt, an egg.

We add chopped onions, lots of cheese,
I use my hands to squish and squeeze!

It's so much fun to mix it all,
Then roll the mixture into balls.

We plop them in the bubbling pot.
The meatballs cook in sauce so hot!

Grandma smiles down at me.
"We're lucky," she says gently.

"One day you'll get to share this too
With a child of your own or two.

You can pass along the recipes
Of your great-grandma from Italy."

Oil

The Glove Family

Part 1

by Andrea Cheng

Mommika Grandma tried to straighten out her fingers. "You know, Annuska, I think I am done knitting," she said. "My fingers just won't do what I tell them anymore."

I looked at Mommika's hands, so knobby at the knuckles. When I was little, she had taught me how to sew dresses for my dolls. Her hands had been sure and strong as we cut the scraps of fabric and shaped them into small dresses and blouses and skirts. We'd even made a Hungarian folk dress with tiny tulips embroidered onto the apron. "You are very good with a needle, Annuska," Mommika had said, smiling.

But now she can hardly bend her fingers. The doctor took x-rays and turned her hands this way and that. Finally he said that Mommika had arthritis. We explained it to her in Hungarian and English. She nodded quietly. She understood.

The doctor said Mommika should keep her hands warm. I made her cups of tea to hold and moved her chair closer to the fire. But her fingers were stiff no matter how much tea I brought.

I wasn't used to seeing Mommika's hands so still. When I came downstairs in the morning, her hands were clasped in her lap. In the evening, Mommika's quiet hands made even her voice stay still.

I tried to help her find her voice. "Mommika, tell me about when you were a little girl in Hungary," I begged, knowing she loved to tell stories. "Tell me about Peti." Usually the stories about Peti were the best, because he was the youngest of Mommika's nine brothers and sisters and he was full of mischief.

"That was so long ago, Annuska," whispered Mommika. "I can barely remember."

This year there were no knitted hats with matching mittens for Christmas, no striped vests or soft sweaters. But I missed Mommika's voice more than those. What about her sister Olga and the time she gave their wax doll a bath in hot water? What about Peti cutting off Zsuzsi's beautiful braids and then hiding them in the closet? Were those words still moving silently in her head?

Mom was sorting through our clothes for spring. Most of my sweaters went to my younger sisters, but some had big holes at the elbows.

"Annuska, take these out to the trash," Mom said. "There's no need to keep worn-out clothes."

I looked sadly at the pile and then picked it up.

Mommika was staring down at her hands, and I startled her as I walked by.

"Wait, Annuska," she said. "Let me see those."

(to be continued)

The Glove Family

Part 2

by Andrea Cheng

I dumped the sweaters next to her rocking chair, and she picked up the blue one on top. She began pulling gently at a piece of yarn near the neck. Soon there was a big mound of curly blue yarn on her lap.

"What are you doing?" I asked.

"Unknitting," Mommika said. "The yarn ends at a hole in a sweater, so you wind it into a ball, like this. Then you can use the yarn to knit something new."

Mommika wrapped yarn around and around her stiff fingers, first in one direction and then the other to keep the ball round. I started a ball of my own. She showed me how to put my fingers underneath the yarn so that when I slipped them out, the ball was soft.

Mommika told me how Peti used to juggle with their mother's yarn balls. "Once he juggled them so high that a yarn ball got stuck in a tree. So he climbed the tree, and threw the ball down on my head," she said, laughing.

I picked up three yarn balls and tried to juggle like Peti. Mommika watched for a minute and then smiled.

After dinner Mommika fell asleep in her chair. Mom came downstairs with an old pair of gloves to add to the pile of sweaters. The gloves gave me an idea. Instead of unknitting them, I sewed up the holes with brown thread. Then I embroidered the faces of Mommika and her brothers and sisters on the fingertips. Peti had bright blue eyes. Zsuzsi had two long braids (before they were cut). Mommika had curly red hair. Just as I finished, Mommika opened her eyes.

"Your family," I said, handing the gloves to her.

"Oh, Annuska! This one must be me," she said, laughing. "And this little pinkie, this must be Peti."

Mommika put the gloves on and told me how she and her brothers and sisters used to race to school in the morning. She moved her fingers back and forth inside the gloves. "Once, I fell, and Ferenc had to carry me the rest of the way." Mommika showed me with her fingers. "Was he mad?"

"Was he ever! But I loved riding piggyback to school." Mommika crossed her fingers.

When Mom brought Mommika her tea, her hands were already warm from the gloves. In fact, she said, they felt nimble. She took off the gloves, picked up her knitting needles and a ball of yarn, and made the first twenty-five stitches of a scarf. "Here, let me show you, Annuska, and we can make it together."

At first my stitches were too loose, but Mommika showed me how to hold the yarn tighter. We were talking and laughing and knitting until way past my bedtime.

"I think I'll sleep with my family gloves on tonight," Mommika said.

"So you'll have your brothers and sisters with you?" I asked.

"Yes. How about you spend the night with all of us in my room?" Mommika suggested, taking my hand in her gloved one as we headed up the stairs.

Objectives
- Model asking questions
- Model determining text importance
- Model summarizing/synthesizing

Review Metacognitive Strategies

Explain to students that readers use multiple metacognitive strategies while they read. Model asking questions, determining text importance, and summarizing/synthesizing. Model integrating these metacognitive strategies before, during, and after reading the selections. Use these questions to encourage students to apply these metacognitive skills.

Ask questions before, during, and after reading.	• Let's look at the illustration. What are you curious about? • What is a question you have about a character, event, idea, or detail? • What questions do you have about the topic now that you have heard this selection?
Determine text importance before, during, and after reading.	• Based on the title, what do you think some big ideas or themes might be in this selection? • What interesting text (dialogue, captions, headers, etc.) did you notice in the selection? • What word or sentence most helped you understand the selection?
Summarize/synthesize before, during, and after reading.	• Can you summarize any prior knowledge you have about this topic? • In general, what just happened in the story? • What was the passage about?

Set the Stage

Introduce the title of the selection. Identify the genre. Note how the selection fits into the theme of observing the sky.

The Moon

Engage Thinking ▶ *What do you know about the moon? Turn and tell a partner.*

Engage with the Text ▶ Read aloud the text at a fluent, expressive pace. Use the suggested prompts to model your thinking, clarify, and elicit student interaction.

1. *I became confused while reading, so I asked myself a question: "Why is the moon this person's special friend?"* (Ask questions)

2. *The last line about wishing to visit the moon really helped me understand why the person is so interested in the moon.* (Determine text importance)

3. *Turn and talk to a partner. Did you develop any new questions about the moon while listening to this poem? If so, share your questions with your partner.* (Ask questions)

A Star's Story

Engage Thinking ▶ *What do you find interesting about stars? Turn and tell a partner.*

Engage with the Text ▶ Read aloud the text at a fluent, expressive pace. Use the suggested prompts to model your thinking, clarify, and elicit student interaction.

1. *This text tells me important facts like how the moon and planets orbit. But the text also has funny words and lines like "whew."* (Determine text importance)

2. *To summarize, our sun is a star that gives off light and heat. The moon reflects this light, and the moon travels around Earth. The Earth and other planets travel around the sun.* (Summarize/synthesize)

3. *Turn and talk to a partner. Did you find any detail in this text particularly interesting? If so, what detail and why?*

Sun, Moon, and Wind Go Out for Dinner

Engage Thinking ▸ *Do you know any stories about the sun and moon? Turn and tell a partner.*

Engage with the Text ▸ Read aloud the text at a fluent, expressive pace. Use the suggested prompts to model your thinking, clarify, and elicit student interaction.

1. *I got confused while reading, so I asked a question: Why did the mother make Sun hot as punishment? To answer my question, I summarized details from the story. Sun ate hot bread. This helped me answer my question.* (Ask questions and summarize/synthesize)

2. *There are a lot of details about the food in Moon's napkin. These are interesting, but not very important. What most helped my understanding of the story is knowing that Moon was generous and brought food for her mother.* (Determine text importance)

3. *Turn and talk to a partner. Retell the story to your partner. If you become confused, stop and ask your partner a question to help you. Then have your partner retell the story and ask you questions when needed.* (Ask questions)

Man in the Moon Mystery Solved

Engage Thinking ▸ *Have you heard about "the man in the moon"? Have you ever drawn a picture of the moon with a face? Turn and tell a partner.*

Engage with the Text ▸ Read aloud the text at a fluent, expressive pace. Use the suggested prompts to model your thinking, clarify, and elicit student interaction.

1. *During the first paragraph, I got confused. I asked myself a question: What is an* asteroid*? I looked it up in a dictionary. An* asteroid *is like a very large piece of rock in space. So scientists thought a very large rock smashed into the moon, creating the face.* (Ask questions)

2. *To better understand the text, sometimes it's helpful to think about the text's big idea, which is that volcanoes on the moon caused the dark spots that look like a face.* (Determine text importance)

3. *Turn and talk to a partner. Take turns asking questions about unknown or confusing words (such as* lava *or* spacecraft*). Answer these questions using context clues or a dictionary.* (Ask questions)

Night Hike

Engage Thinking ▸ *Have you ever walked around outside during a full moon? What was it like to use the light of the moon to see? Turn and tell a partner.*

Engage with the Text ▸ Read aloud the text at a fluent, expressive pace. Use the suggested prompts to model your thinking, clarify, and elicit student interaction.

1. *While reading, I had a question: Would Abeni be scared in the dark? Then I read that the moonlight was bright and she was not scared, so this answered my question.* (Ask questions)

2. *I can summarize the story to deepen my understanding: Abeni and her uncle Obi go on a night hike during a full moon and use the moonlight to see special animals, flowers, and insects.* (Summarize/synthesize)

3. *Turn and talk to a partner. Imagine you went on the night hike. What questions would you have for Abeni or Uncle Obi? Share your questions with each other.* (Ask questions)

Unit 8

CCSS:

RL.1.1, RL.1.2, RL.1.3, RI.1.1, RI.1.2, RI.1.3, SL.1.1, SL.1.2

The Moon

by Mary Harvey

Every night I go outside
And look up at the sky.
I see my special friend, the moon.
We tell each other "Hi."

The moon and I, we go way back
To my very early days.
"Moon" was the first word
I ever learned to say!

The moon, it watches over me
And keeps me safe all night.
When I see it through my window
I know everything's all right.

I ask the moon my questions:
"What will tomorrow bring?"
I tell the moon my secrets:
"Shh! Don't ever say a thing!"

It changes shape, a sight to see.
I watch it day by day.
It becomes a tiny sliver,
Then for a short time goes away.

But then it grows and grows again
So big and bright and round.
The full moon is my favorite sight
From down here on the ground.

I stand outside and look up high.
It takes my breath away.
The moon, it knows my greatest wish:
To visit it someday.

Unit 8

A Star's Story

by Rachel Young

Hello, everyone. I'm here with Stella the star, reporting live from outer space. Whew, Stella, it sure is hot out here.

Well, we stars are known for being fiery. We're like giant power plants giving off light and heat and energy.

Giant? But from Earth you look so tiny compared with the sun and moon.

That's because I'm so far away. Actually, I'm a much bigger star than the sun. Your sun only looks big because it's the closest star to Earth. As for the moon, it's even closer to Earth, but it's just a little hunk of rock, not a star!

A rock? Is that the truth?

Of course, darling! Without the sun, the moon wouldn't be much to look at. Did you know it doesn't shine at all? That dusty rock only reflects the sun's light, just like a mirror.

And all this time I thought the moon was shining too.

Everyone does. Poor little moon, always running around in circles. I'm so glad that I don't have to orbit.

Or what?

Orbit. A moon circles around its planet in a path called an orbit. Planets orbit too, but they travel around a star. Why, it takes a whole year for Earth to orbit around the sun! How exhausting. I'm so glad we stars get to stay put.

That sounds a little lazy to me.

We might not move, but stars are always working. Without starlight, your planet would be cold and dark—a real party pooper. Light from the sun warms Earth so that it's just the right temperature for plants, animals, and people.

Thank you, I guess.

No need for thanks, darling. Lighting up the lives of all you little people is reward enough for me.

Sun, Moon, and Wind Go Out for Dinner

(A Fairy Tale from India)

One evening Sun, Moon, and Wind were very hungry. They wanted dinner. But their mother—one of the most beautiful stars in the entire sky—was not feeling well. She was too ill to cook. So instead Sun, Moon, and Wind traveled to the home of their Uncle Thunder and Aunt Lightning.

Their uncle and aunt had prepared a huge feast for them! A large table was covered with the most delicious foods. There was warm bread and roasted meats. There were fresh fruits and vegetables. And there were the sweetest desserts. As soon as Sun saw the bread and meats, he ran straight to the table. He started eating. As soon as Wind saw the desserts, she also ran straight to the table. She ate as much of the creams and puddings as she could. Neither Sun nor Wind thought about sharing.

But Moon was different. She greeted her aunt and uncle. Then she sat down at the table. She ate with her aunt and uncle. They talked. They shared whatever food was left with each other. When dinner was over, Moon kindly thanked them both.

When Sun, Moon, and Wind got home, they went straight to see their mother. Their mother was in bed. Although sick, she was happy to see her children.

"My children," their mother said, "what did you bring home for me to eat?"

Sun replied, "Nothing. Uncle Thunder and Aunt Lightning do not know how to have a feast. There was barely enough food for us children. Definitely not enough food to bring home to you, too." This, of course, was a lie.

Then Wind said, "I'm sorry, Mother. I did not bring you any food. I knew you were sick. But Uncle Thunder and Aunt Lightning only had desserts. I knew sweets would make you feel worse." This too, of course, was a lie.

Lastly, Moon spoke. She said, "Here, Mother. Uncle Thunder and Aunt Lightning made many good things. I brought you back some fine food. I know it is not much. But it is all I could carry." Then she took a napkin from her pocket. She opened the napkin up. First, there were a few green beans. Then a piece of tender meat. Moon kept opening up the napkin. And there was more and more food for her mother. There was a hunk of bread. Then a few strawberries. And lastly, a fine slice of cake.

"What a wonderful meal," exclaimed her mother. She smiled down on Moon. Then she turned to Sun and Wind.

"Sun!" she yelled. "You went out. You ate hot meats. You filled yourself up on warm bread. You think only of yourself. You never thought of your mother. So from now on, you will be cursed! You will be hot to the touch. You will be scorching. You will release such heat that none of your friends can come too close. All people will cover their heads when they see you.

"Wind!" she yelled. "You went out. You ate whipped creams. You ate fluffy puddings. You also never thought about your mother. So now, you will also be cursed. From now on, you will whip the winds. You will cause dangerous storms. You will blow harsh air across the lands. All people will run from you.

"Moon!" said their mother. "You were different. You remembered your mother. You were kind. You were generous. You shared your food. From now on, you will brighten up the dark skies. Whenever you appear, people will look at you with love. They will be joyful at the sight of you. Around the world, people will feel grateful for you."

Unit 8

Man in the Moon Mystery Solved

Scientists think they know why the moon's surface has dark shapes.

by Russell Kahn, News-O-Matic, October 2, 2014

The surface of the moon has huge dark areas. Many people see a face of a man in the shapes. For years, scientists thought an asteroid created the "man in the moon." Recently, they announced a new idea.

So, what created the dark spot called Oceanus Procellarum? It wasn't a space rock slamming into the moon. It was probably a huge volcano! It flooded the moon with lava about four billion years ago. That created the dark rock we see today.

Two spacecraft helped make the discovery. The pair, named GRAIL, studied the moon's shape and surface. Scientists noticed that the dark area was not the right shape. If an asteroid crashed into it, the shape would be a circle. But its shape was a rectangle!

Maria Zuber from Cambridge, Massachusetts, was an author of the report. She told the *Washington Post* that it was a great discovery. "For anyone who's ever looked up at the moon and wondered why it has this pattern—now we have an answer."

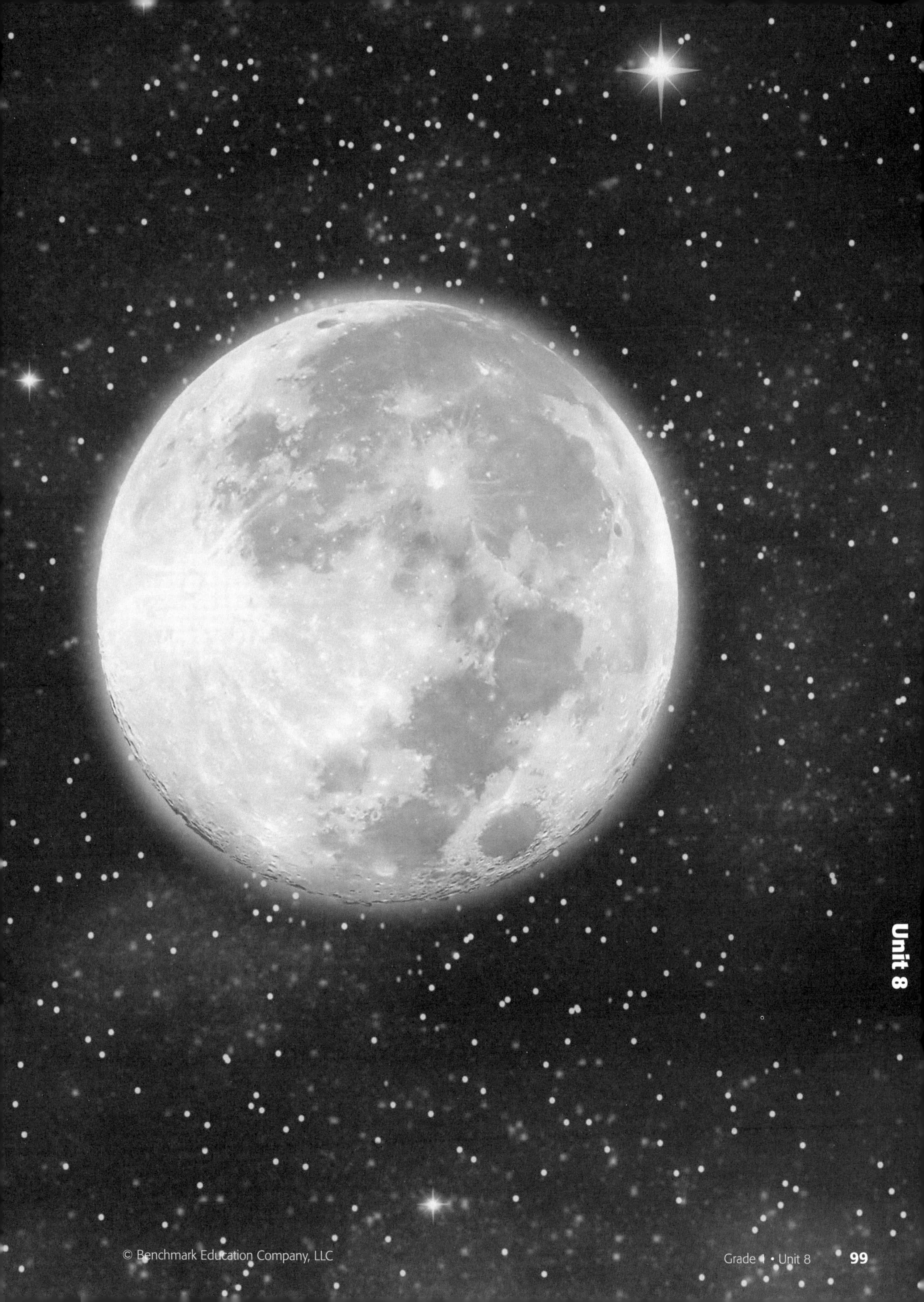

Unit 8

Night Hike

The clock said it was 7:45 p.m. It was almost time for bed. Abeni could hardly wait. Tonight she did not have to go to bed at 8 o'clock. Tonight was special. She and Uncle Obi were going on a night hike.

Abeni lived in a city in California. But Uncle Obi lived near a big forest. He knew so much about the forest! He knew about the animals that lived there. He knew all the names of the plants that grew there. And he knew the best time to go on a night hike.

Last week Uncle Obi had come over for dinner. He asked Abeni's mom if Abeni could come with him on a night hike.

"We will see all kinds of things that we cannot see in the daytime," said Uncle Obi. "Owls, for instance. And bats. Those are two animals that come out at night. We might even see some flowers that open only at night."

Abeni's mom had agreed to let Abeni go with Uncle Obi. Abeni could not wait. She wanted to go that night.

"We have to wait for the full moon," Uncle Obi told Abeni. "That is when the moon is the brightest. It will give us light. That way we can see lots of things."

So Abeni had waited a whole week. Finally it was time. She was wearing her boots and her warm coat. In her backpack were a snack and a flashlight. She was ready.

"Ready to go?" asked Uncle Obi when he came to pick her up.

"Ready!" said Abeni.

They drove to the forest. Soon they reached the start of the trail. Abeni could not see anything. She reached for her flashlight. She was about to turn it on.

"Wait a second, Abeni," said Uncle Obi. "Look up. What do you see?"

Abeni looked up at the night sky. She saw hundreds of stars. They were twinkling brightly. Abeni saw so many more stars here than at home. And they seemed brighter than the ones she saw at home.

"Now look up and to the right," said Uncle Obi. "What do you see there?"

Shining in the sky was the biggest, brightest moon Abeni had ever seen. It gave off so much light. She thought she could even see a face in the moon. She remembered that she had read once about the "man in the moon." That face must be what people thought looked like a man.

"I wanted us to wait for a full moon for our hike," said Uncle Obi. "That way we would not have to use our flashlights. The moon will give us enough light to see where we are going. We will still keep our flashlights with us, just in case. Look carefully at the forest. I promise you we will see many special things. The light of the moon will guide us."

Abeni looked at the forest in front of them. She stood quietly and waited. She heard a hooting coming from a tree. She looked in the tree and saw a large barn owl. It was watching them.

She looked down at the ground. She saw plants with small white flowers. She even saw a bug with hundreds of legs.

"What are we waiting for?" Abeni asked Uncle Obi. "The moon is showing us the way. Let's get going!"

We Use Goods and Services

Objectives
- Model visualizing
- Model making inferences and predictions
- Model making connections

Review Metacognitive Strategies

Explain to students that readers use multiple metacognitive strategies while they read. Model visualizing, making inferences and predictions, and making connections. Model integrating these metacognitive strategies before, during, and after reading the selections. Use these questions to encourage students to apply these metacognitive skills.

Visualize before, during, and after reading.	• What images come to mind when you hear the title? • What words helped you picture the characters, events, and ideas? • How did the words and phrases make you feel?
Make inferences and predictions before, during, and after reading.	• Based on the title and illustration, what do you think will happen? • Why did the character act this way? • What do you think will happen next? Why?
Make connections before, during, and after reading.	• Have you ever experienced anything like what we just read about? If so, what? • Did this remind you of anything else you've read? If so, what? • Could this happen in our world today? Why or why not?

Set the Stage

Introduce the title of the selection. Identify the genre. Note how the selection fits into the theme of how we use goods and services.

Real Jobs! Apple Farmer

Engage Thinking ▶ *What job would you like to have when you grow up? Turn and tell a partner.*

Engage with the Text ▶ Read aloud the text at a fluent, expressive pace. Use the suggested prompts to model your thinking, clarify, and elicit student interaction.

1. *Debbie says, "We need to be around in case bad weather comes." I pictured a person working in a snowstorm. Based on this, I decided that apple picking is a tough job.* (Visualize and make inferences/predictions)

2. *Debbie said they get special "short" trees that are easier to pick. I once picked apples from these short trees, and it was easier!* (Make connections)

3. *Turn and talk to a partner. How does Debbie make money? What does Debbie use the money to pay for in order to run the farm?*

No More, No Less, Part 1

Engage Thinking ▶ *Why do people save their money? Turn and tell a partner.*

Engage with the Text ▶ Read aloud the text at a fluent, expressive pace. Use the suggested prompts to model your thinking, clarify, and elicit student interaction.

1. *When I read that Leib buries his money, I pictured him digging in the dirt in the dark. This made me think about my piggy bank, which I think is better than putting money in the ground.* (Visualize and make connections)

2. *When Leib sees the house, I think he figures out that someone in the house must have stolen his money. So I predict that he will try to get his money back.* (Make inferences/predictions).

3. *Turn and talk to a partner. What is Leib hoping to buy with the money?*

No More, No Less, Part 2

Engage Thinking ▶ *Think about the first part of the story. What happened to Leib's money? Turn and tell a partner.*

Engage with the Text ▶ Read aloud the text at a fluent, expressive pace. Use the suggested prompts to model your thinking, clarify, and elicit student interaction.

1. *When the old man smiles, I pictured a sneaky smile because I think the old man is planning to steal more of Leib's money.* (Visualize and make inferences/predictions)

2. *When the old man puts the money back, this made me think Leib is really smart to come up with such a good trick. This reminds me of my brother, who is really good at tricks and pranks.* (Make connections)

3. *Turn and talk to a partner. If you had a lot of money like Leib, what would you do with it? Would you save it, spend it, or hide it? Why?*

Market Day

Engage Thinking ▶ *Have you ever traded anything you own for something else? Turn and tell a partner.*

Engage with the Text ▶ Read aloud the text at a fluent, expressive pace. Use the suggested prompts to model your thinking, clarify, and elicit student interaction.

1. *I pictured Balam with a few tiny beans and small feathers. So I figured he would not be able to buy much. But then he buys a copper necklace. This made me realize that cacao beans and quetzal feathers must be worth a lot.* (Visualize and make inferences/predictions)

2. *The busy market in the story reminds me of going to a farmers' market with my mother.* (Make connections)

3. *Turn and talk to a partner. What is something you own that you think would be worth a lot in a trade? Why?*

Traders

Engage Thinking ▶ *Why do people trade with each other? How does trading help them? Turn and tell a partner.*

Engage with the Text ▶ Read aloud the text at a fluent, expressive pace. Use the suggested prompts to model your thinking, clarify, and elicit student interaction.

1. *When I read or listen to a poem, I think about how it makes me feel. When I hear phrases like happy sound and shaking all around, it makes me feel happy too. Which words and phrases in this poem make you feel happy?* (Visualize and make connections)

2. *At the end, I predict that the child will not trade the yo-yo because the child doesn't seem to miss the dinosaur.* (Make inferences/prediction)

3. *Turn and talk to a partner. Tell how different parts of the poem make you feel. Which words and phrases gave you that feeling?*

CCSS:

RL.1.1, RL.1.3, RI.1.1, RI.1.3, SL.1.1, SL.1.2, SL.1.4

Unit 9

Real Jobs! Apple Farmer

by Abigail Mieko Vargus, News-O-Matic, October 8, 2014

In much of the United States, October means more than changing leaves. It is a time to pick apples! News-O-Matic talked to Debbie Auger (DA), an orchardist in Littleton, Massachusetts. She told us what it's like to grow and sell apples at Nagog Hill Orchard.

What is your job?

DA: I'm the president of Nagog Fruiters. I run the farm stand, make sure we have plenty of fruits and vegetables to offer, and go to farmers' markets around the state. I also pay the workers and run errands for the farm.

What do you grow?

DA: We have about 30 varieties of apple trees. We also have peach, plum, pear, and nectarine trees, plus lots of vegetables. My favorite apples are Macoun (muh-KOWN) and Honeycrisp.

How do you choose what to grow?

DA: My husband, Charles, is in charge of the growing. Apple trees can live over 40 years, but we lose some every year to weather, illness, or just old age. He chooses the new trees. When they come, they just look like sticks! Sometimes we get special trees that are short, so it's easier to pick.

What's it like running a farm stand?

DA: The most important thing is to build relationships with my customers. I smile and make them feel welcome. It's all about treating each other with respect and kindness.

That sounds like fun! Is it ever hard?

DA: It can be. Sometimes customers can be grumpy or rude. I have a sign in the farm stand that says, "Be Nice or Go Away." But usually I love it. The only thing I don't like about farming is that I never get to go anywhere. We always need to be here, taking care of the farm.

Can't you go away in winter or spring?

DA: Our farm stand isn't year-round, but we are always working. In winter, we prune the trees, which prepares them for spring. In spring, we get the trees ready for their blossoms. We need to be around in case bad weather comes too.

What happens if there's bad weather?

DA: We do our best to save the trees and fruit. If you lose a lot of your crop, you have to tighten your belt and you have to hope next year is better. But it's worth it.

What is it like on the farm?

DA: It's peaceful on a farm. We're on a hill, so we call it our little piece of heaven. We get to see double rainbows and beautiful sunsets.

Is it fun?

DA: Absolutely. In the fall, we package apples for gift boxes. Sometimes we have to package 500 boxes in just two days! It sounds overwhelming. But when you have a lot of people and you're listening to music, it's a lot of fun.

Do you ever get tired of apples?

DA: Yes! By the end of the season, I'm so tired of looking at apples that I don't want to see another until next year.

What would you tell a kid who wants to run an orchard someday?

DA: Go to an agricultural college to learn all about plants and trees. And be willing to work hard. It's a warrior's job.

Unit 9

No More, No Less
A Polish Folktale, Part 1
retold by Marci Stillerman

Many years ago, in the small Polish town of Pinchow, there lived a trader named Leib. He worked hard, but times were bad. He never had enough money to buy presents for his children or a silk dress for his beloved wife, Sonya. Sometimes he couldn't even buy food or wood to burn in the stove to keep them warm.

One bitterly cold winter day, Leib made an important decision. He would leave home for the big city of Krakow. Maybe he could earn more money there. He gave his wife all the money he had and, with a heavy heart, said good-bye to her and his children.

In Krakow, Leib poured all of his energy into his work and had amazing success. After twelve months, he had 600 *zlotys* jingling in his purse.

God has been good to me, he thought. I have earned more money in one year than in the whole of my life.

But every day, he missed his family more. He was nearly sick from longing for them. "I cannot go on another day without Sonya and my children," he said and decided to go home. He already had enough money to take care of them for a very long time.

On his way home, Leib stopped in the town of Rozka. He was weary and needed to rest. Fearing there might be robbers in the town, he decided to bury his money before going to the inn. Near a small wooden house that seemed to be deserted, he dug a hole and, looking around to make sure no one saw him, buried his money.

But the house was not deserted. The old man who owned it was watching through his window. When Leib left for the inn, the old man went out and dug it up. He laughed at the stupid stranger who would bury 600 *zlotys* in the ground and trust that no one would find it.

Next morning, when Leib went to get his money, it was gone. Tears came to his eyes. "I have never had money to buy presents for my wife and children. Now when I have earned enough to take care of them, am I to have lost it all?"

Looking around sadly, he noticed the nearby house.

(to be continued)

No More, No Less

A Polish Folktale, Part 2

retold by Marci Stillerman

Whoever lives in that house must have seen me bury the money, Leib thought. But if I accuse him of stealing it, he will call me a liar.

Leib went to the house and knocked on the door.

"Peace be with you," he said to the old man. "I am a stranger here and need advice. The innkeeper told me you are the wisest man in town. Will you help me?"

The old man was flattered. "Tell me what I can do to help you," he said.

"Fearing robbers, I buried my money—600 *zlotys*—in a secret place when I came to your town last night," Leib said. "Now I have received 1,000 *zlotys* in payment of a debt. I left it in my room at the inn while I decide what to do with it for safekeeping. Should I bury it in the same secret place or in another for the greatest safety?"

The old man smiled.

"Since you are a stranger here, it would be best to have all your money in the same place. I advise you to bury it there. Go at night so no one will see you."

"Thank you for your advice," said Leib. "I will do as you suggest."

As soon as Leib was out of sight, the old man took the purse of money he had stolen and hurried to where he'd dug it up the night before.

If the foolish man comes to his hiding place and doesn't find his money, he'll bury his 1,000 *zlotys* far from here,' the greedy man said to himself. If he finds his money where he left it, he will think it safe to bury the 1,000 *zlotys* in the same place, and I will get all his money.

When darkness fell, Leib went to the hiding place and found all his stolen money. Not a single *zloty* was missing.

"The old fellow thought he would get more, and now he has less." Leib laughed quietly. "It is no more nor less than he deserves."

On his way home, Leib bought presents for his family. In a few hours' time, he was sitting cozily by the fire at home. His children played with their new toys by the hearth, and his wife looked lovelier than ever in her new silk dress. Leib leaned back in his chair and closed his eyes as a contented smile spread across his face.

Unit 9

Market Day

by Sydney Salter Husseman

"Hurry, Balam!"

I struggled to catch up with my father. My neck ached from carrying the heavy basket of salt. Why did my brother get to carry the feathers? Thousands of people filled the canoes that would take us to the great Aztec market of Tlatelolco (tlah-tell-OHL-co).

When we arrived, my father gave me a handful of cacao beans and ten quetzal (ket-ZAHL) feathers. "Buy a gift for your baby sister," he told me. He and my brother went to trade jaguar furs, salt, feathers, and cloth for swords and copper axes.

The air smelled like ripe fruit, incense, and cooking. My stomach rumbled. I passed rows of avocados, beans, chilies, peanuts, pineapples, potatoes, squash, and tomatoes, a rainbow of colors. Next to a pile of turkeys, I spotted someone selling tamales (tah-MAHL-ace). I spent one cacao bean on my tasty snack.

I had never seen so many people from so many places. Some women wore their hair like little horns on top of their head; others had teeth stained red or black. A few people had lip and nose plugs. One man had jade in his teeth like my father did. Some people painted their faces, and others had tattoos. I saw clothes of every color and pattern.

I followed the sound of music through rows of baskets, clay pots, and little clay figures. People were listening to a man singing a story to the rhythm of a flute and a wooden gong.

A fight erupted at a nearby stand. Someone had tried to buy cloth with dirt-filled cacao beans. The market officers hustled the man to court.

I spent the rest of my cacao beans on a cup of chocolate. The quetzal feathers would be enough to buy my sister's gift. I wanted to get her something special, something that could be found only at the great Aztec market of Tlatelolco. I walked past sellers of jade, gold, feather jewelry, pottery, and slaves. And then I saw it: a necklace made of tiny copper beads. It was the perfect gift for my sister.

Traders

I got a brand-new treasure,
A brand-new toy dinosaur.
I could hold it in my fingers
And imagine its big roar.

I played with it awhile
Until I spotted Jade.
She had a fancy yo-yo,
And I asked if we could trade.

Jade gave me the yo-yo,
And she took the dinosaur.
It was great for her collection—
Just what she was looking for.

Then Jade saw Yoshie down the street.
What was Yoshie playing with?
A shiny little bouncy ball.
Jade could not resist.

"If you give me your ball," she said,
"You can have this dinosaur.
I know the ball is lots of fun,
but you might like this more."

Yoshie took the dino.
Then she heard a happy sound.
Owen had a tambourine
He was shaking all around.

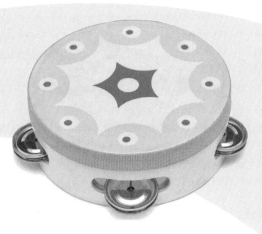

"I really like that," Yoshie said.
"I'll trade my dinosaur.
It's fierce and green and scaly
Like you've never seen before."

Owen played with his new prize,
As happy as could be.
It was the best toy ever,
And he wanted me to see.

When Owen came to show me,
He saw me flicking my yo-yo.
"Say, how'd you like to trade," he said.
"I've something new, you know."

He opened up his fingers,
And there was my dinosaur.
The very one I'd traded
To someone else before.

He said, "I got this dino
For my little tambourine.
Isn't it the coolest thing
that you have ever seen?"

Unit 9

Unit 10

Exploring Sound and Light

Objectives
• Model asking questions
• Model determining text importance
• Model using fix-up monitoring strategies

Review Metacognitive Strategies

Explain to students that readers use multiple metacognitive strategies while they read. Model asking questions, determining text importance, and using fix-up monitoring strategies. Model integrating these metacognitive strategies before, during, and after reading the selections. Use these questions to encourage students to apply these metacognitive skills.

Ask questions before, during, and after reading.	• Let's look at the illustration. What are you curious about? • What questions do you have about a character, event, idea, or detail? • What questions do you have about the topic now that you have heard this selection?
Determine text importance before, during, and after reading.	• Based on the title, what do you think some big ideas or themes might be in this selection? • What interesting text (dialogue, captions, headers, etc.) did you notice in the selection? • What details were most important to understanding the selection?
Use fix-up monitoring strategies before, during, and after reading.	• Let's read the title and look at the illustration. What do you find confusing? • What is a detail that confused you? Let's read ahead to figure it out. • Did any part of the selection confuse you? If so, let's reread that part.

Set the Stage

Introduce the title of the selection. Identify the genre. Note how the selection fits into the theme of sound and light.

Lightning

Engage Thinking ▶ *What do you know about lightning? Turn and tell a partner.*

Engage with the Text ▶ Read aloud the text at a fluent, expressive pace. Use the suggested prompts to model your thinking, clarify, and elicit student interaction.

1. *How does this poem make me feel at the beginning? It makes me feel a little scared. What words and phrases make me feel that way? It is words and phrases like "frightening,"0. and "tearing up."* (Ask questions)

2. *Some words were confusing, like* thwacking *and* squall*. But I can tell from other details in the poem that these words are describing the storm and the lightning.* (Use fix-up monitoring strategies)

3. *Turn and talk to a partner. How does it make you feel? Ask your partner questions about what words and phrases make him or her feel that way.* (Ask questions)

Signing, Not Singing!

Engage Thinking ▶ *How would life be different without sound? How would you talk to others? Turn and tell a partner.*

Engage with the Text ▶ Read aloud the text at a fluent, expressive pace. Use the suggested prompts to model your thinking, clarify, and elicit student interaction.

1. *I didn't understand what ASL was, so I reread the passage. Then I saw that ASL means American Sign Language. So now I understand that Adams teaches sign language.* (Use fix-up monitoring strategies)

2. *At the end, I had a question: Are the videos for everyone or for people who cannot hear?* (Ask questions)

3. *Turn and talk to a partner. If you could talk to Brittany Adams, what questions would you ask her? Share your questions with your partner.* (Ask questions)

The Ojibwa jingle dress

Engage Thinking ▸ *Have you ever heard the sound of tiny bells? Turn and tell a partner.*

Engage with the Text ▸ Read aloud the text at a fluent, expressive pace. Use the suggested prompts to model your thinking, clarify, and elicit student interaction.

1. *I wondered how a jingle dress could cure the granddaughter. So I reread. Kathryn said dancing in her dress made her feel good. So perhaps the dress made the granddaughter feel good.* (Ask questions and use fix-up monitoring strategies)

2. *The details describing the sound of the jingle dress ("metal cones" and "sound like rain") helped me understand the dress the most.* (Determine text importance)

3. *Turn and talk to a partner. Imagine hearing many people dancing in jingle dresses. How does this make you feel?*

The Sweetest Melody

Engage Thinking ▸ *What is your favorite song? What is your favorite sound? Turn and tell a partner.*

Engage with the Text ▸ Read aloud the text at a fluent, expressive pace. Use the suggested prompts to model your thinking, clarify, and elicit student interaction.

1. *I had a question about one of the characters as I read. I asked myself: Why does the shah send all his advisers out of the room?* (Ask questions)

2. *I don't know what an adviser is, but I understand that the shah is asking people questions. So I can still understand the story without knowing that word.* (Use fix-up monitoring strategies and determine text importance)

3. *Turn and talk to a partner. Ask your partner a question about the character Merza Zaki. See if your partner can answer your question using details from the story. Then have your partner ask you a question and try to answer it with details from the story.* (Ask questions)

Firefly Dance

Engage Thinking ▸ *Have you seen fireflies? What do they look like? Turn and tell a partner.*

Engage with the Text ▸ Read aloud the text at a fluent, expressive pace. Use the suggested prompts to model your thinking, clarify, and elicit student interaction.

1. *I didn't understand the line "in hands held tight," so I reread the poem. Now I realize that the poem is talking about ways of capturing fireflies.* (Ask questions and use fix-up monitoring strategies)

2. *The rhyming words in the poem (flight/tight/light/night) are important because the rhyme helps me feel the music of the fireflies dancing.* (Determine text importance)

3. *Turn and talk to a partner. How does the poem make you feel about the light from fireflies? What words and phrases suggest those feelings?*

CCSS:

RL.1.1, RL.1.2, RL.1.3, RI.1.1, RI.1.2, SL.1.1, SL.1.2

Unit 10

Lightning

by Jennifer Jesseph

I see lightning,
and it's frightening,
tearing up the summer skies.

Watch it flashing.
See it slashing.
Everything electrifies.

Hear it cracking.
Trees are thwacking.
I curl into a ball.

I cover my head,
and stay in bed
away from this big squall.

Now it's slowing.
The storm is going.
The lightning's not so bright.

It's getting dimmer,
just a glimmer
of flickering, flashing light.

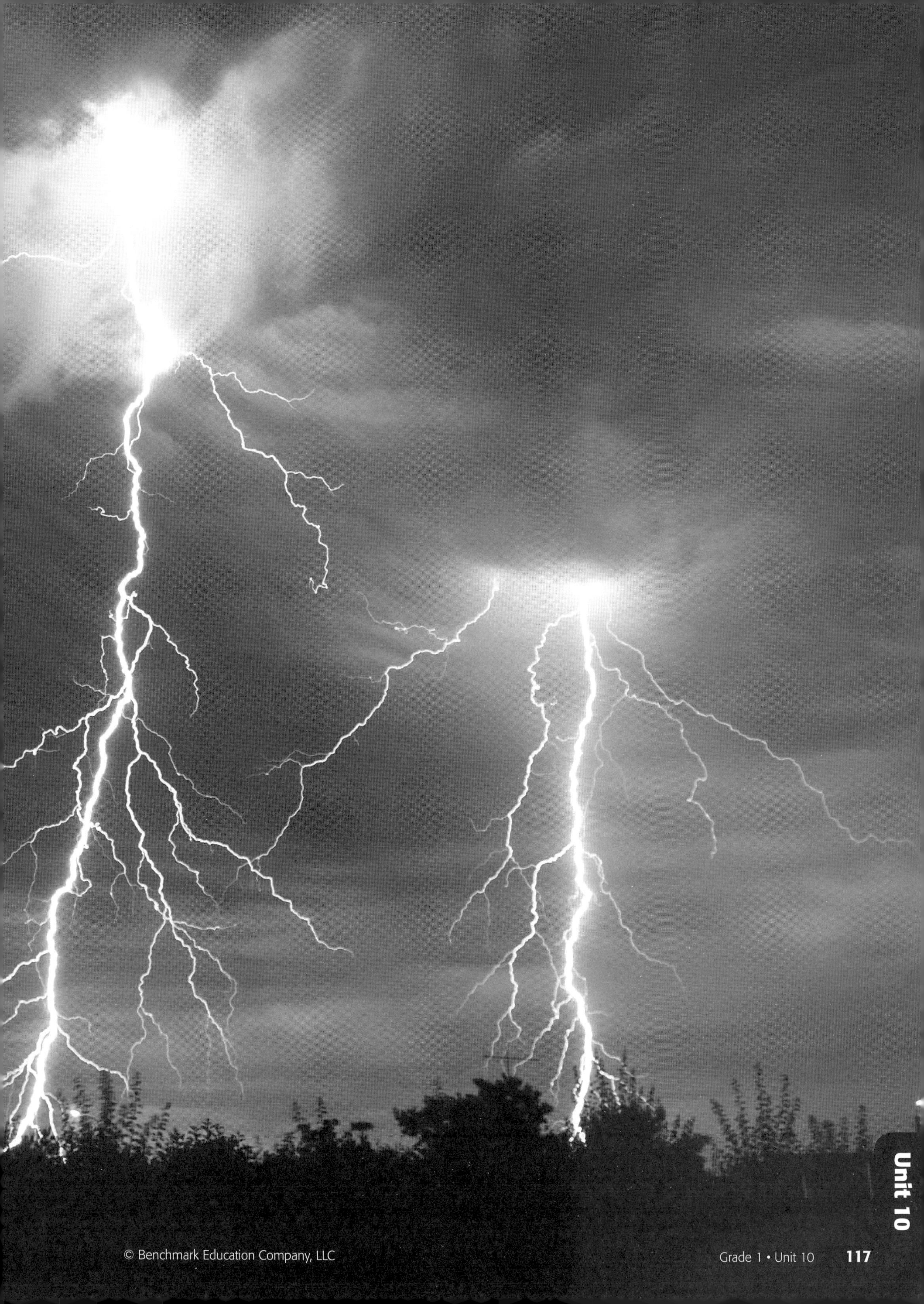

Unit 10

Signing, Not Singing!

A teacher uses Taylor Swift music to help her class learn sign language!

by Stephanie Santana, News-O-Matic, October 2, 2014

Teacher Brittany Adams loves to make her lessons pop. What better way than to use pop music? Adams makes music videos to teach sign language. She used a Taylor Swift song for one!

People who cannot hear use American Sign Language (ASL) to communicate. Adams teaches ASL in Romeo, Michigan. That lets her hearing students connect with people who are deaf. She made the videos to excite kids about the language!

"I wanted people to see ASL the way I do," said Adams. And Adams sure makes it look fun! In her video, people are shaking it to Swift's "Shake It Off." Meanwhile, Adams signs every word of the song.

Swift's song plays in Adams's video. You can turn the volume off to see how a deaf person sees it. Adams's students loved the video. And they are thrilled to get to make their own videos this year.

It looks like adding that pop worked!

The Ojibwa jingle dress

by Clinton Elliott, Ojibwa

The jingle dress is a gift from the Ojibwa people, who come from the Great Lakes. The dress is made with lots of metal cones. They are called jingles. The jingles sound like rain falling softly on a roof. jingle dresses are very pretty. Read on to discover the true story of the jingle dress.

"Hi, my name is Kathryn Elaine Stalk. I'm Ojibwa/Mohawk. My father is Ojibwa, and my mother is Mohawk. I dance at powwows. I have on my very own jingle dress. My daddy gave it to me. I just love it. It's yellow, my favorite color. When I put on my jingle dress, I dance softly as the wind. Lots of my friends and I go to powwows on weekends with our parents. We stay overnight. We bring Grandma along. It's good to have powwows. I see my aunts and uncles there and meet new friends. Powwows make me feel good about being Indian."

The Story of the jingle dress

Once an Ojibwa grandfather searched the countryside for a cure for his beautiful granddaughter.

She was very sick and near death. He loved her so very much. He wanted her to live. One night, the grandfather had a dream. In the dream, the spirits came to him. They told him about a jingle dress. They showed him how to make one. They said if he made one for his granddaughter, she would get well and dance gently as the wind. He returned home at once. At home, he helped Grandma sew together the jingle dress for their granddaughter.

When the sick granddaughter saw the jingle dress, her eyes opened slowly. Then, they opened wide. She sat up and smiled. She knew the jingle dress would help her. She could not wait to put it on. She was very, very happy! As soon as she had it on, she began to dance. She knew all the steps without being told, they just came naturally. It was like a brand-new day. The granddaughter was cured of her sickness. She lived for a very long time.

This is why the jingle dress is a healing dress. The Ojibwa people share it with everyone. They say that the jingle dress is for all women who want to heal.

The Sweetest Melody
(A Folktale from Afghanistan)
adapted by Lydia Nearing

Long ago, there lived a shah of Persia who was curious about the world and often thought in riddles.

One day the shah was holding court with four of his advisers, discussing grand ideas and hard questions. "What is the sweetest melody?" he suddenly asked.

The first adviser answered, "Without question, the melody of the flute is the sweetest. It trills like a bird in a blossoming tree."

The second adviser spoke up. "No, no, you have it all wrong. The melody of the harp is by far the sweetest. It sounds just like the music that is played in heaven."

The third adviser butted in. "You are both barking up the wrong tree. In all of the universe, the melody of the guitar has the finest tone. It can play loudly and boldly. It can play softly and gently. When a man hears it, he feels as if someone were strumming his own heart."

The three advisers looked at the shah to find out which of them was right. But the shah was looking at his fourth adviser, Merza Zaki, who sat very still and said nothing. The shah sent them all from the room.

Several days passed. Then Merza Zaki invited the shah and the other advisers to a banquet in their honor. That evening, the finest musicians in the land entertained them on all types of instruments.

"How strange," the advisers noticed. "There is a table here but no refreshments." (Usually at these banquets, the tables are filled with special foods: raisins and olives, dates and oranges, meats and rice—even when the guests have eaten their fill, still more food is carried out.)

But this night was different. Though the music was rich, the table was bare. Where was the food? The guests' stomachs began to rumble with hunger. "We've been here for hours!" they thought to themselves. "We shall starve." It was nearly midnight. And still they waited.

Finally, Merza Zaki called for the headwaiter, who entered the room banging a silver ladle on the lid of a huge pot of steaming food. The sound rang through the silent room like a great bell.

All the guests smiled in relief. Suddenly, the shah spoke up in excitement. "The clink of dishes in the ears of a hungry person—this is the sweetest melody," he said to Merza Zaki. "That is the answer."

Firefly Dance

by Lindsay Koch

Like fairies in flight,
Like grounded stars
In hands held tight
Or captured in jars.
Tiny lanterns of living light:
Fireflies keeping watch in the night.

Their wings whirring
In gentle flight
Set the air stirring—
A bowl of light.
Summer night spangled and tangled in gold,
Fireflies to catch, magic to hold.

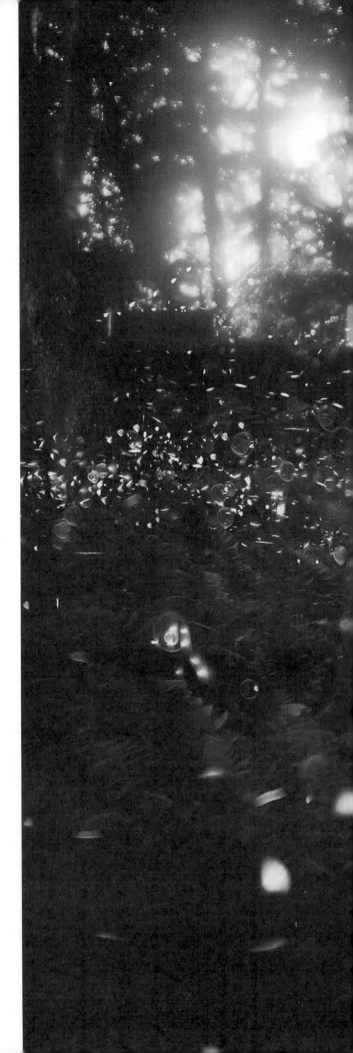

Unit 10

Grade 1 Passage Matrix

Unit	Unit Topic	Title	Author/Source
1	Being a Good Community Member	New School for Hopperville	Click magazine
1	Being a Good Community Member	Surfing for Change	Stephanie Santana
1	Being a Good Community Member	Voting Day	Mary Harvey
1	Being a Good Community Member	The Free and the Brave	Ariella Tievsky
1	Being a Good Community Member	A Visit to the Library	Tori Telfer
2	Many Kinds of Characters	Feathers Fall from Trees	Carol Brendler
2	Many Kinds of Characters	Climb Aboard the Merry-Go-Round	Cara Brooks
2	Many Kinds of Characters	Who Lives There?	Carolyn Matt Ford
2	Many Kinds of Characters	Curious	Mary Harvey
2	Many Kinds of Characters	The Kite	Valeri Gorbachev
3	Plants and Animals Grow and Change	Changes	Edna Ledgard
3	Plants and Animals Grow and Change	A Dad Who Has Babies	Marilyn Singer
3	Plants and Animals Grow and Change	Sunflower	Tony Mancus
3	Plants and Animals Grow and Change	Why Do Animals Play?	Kathleen Weidner Zoehfeld
3	Plants and Animals Grow and Change	Why Opossum's Tail Is Bare	Sherine Gilmour
4	Stories Have a Narrator	Where My Aunt Rose Lives	Eileen Spinelli
4	Stories Have a Narrator	Purr Baby, Part 1	Karmen Kooyers
4	Stories Have a Narrator	Purr Baby, Part 2	Karmen Kooyers
4	Stories Have a Narrator	City Tug, Country Tug	Charlotte Pomerantz
4	Stories Have a Narrator	In the Beginning of Time	Sherine Gilmour
5	Technology at Work	Alien Alert	Olive Evans
5	Technology at Work	A Special Bag	Ariella Tievsky
5	Technology at Work	Operation: Rescue Possum	Charnan Simon
5	Technology at Work	New Power for Vermont City!	Liz Lane
5	Technology at Work	Where's Taro?	Ariella Tievsky
6	Stories Teach Many Lessons	Sticking with It	Tony Mancus
6	Stories Teach Many Lessons	Throwing Beans	Suzanne Kamata
6	Stories Teach Many Lessons	Good-Bye, Training Wheels	Maggie Moran
6	Stories Teach Many Lessons	The Man Who Never Lied	Sherine Gilmour
6	Stories Teach Many Lessons	Oops!	Mary Harvey
7	Past, Present, and Future	Pieces of the Past	Ariella Tievsky
7	Past, Present, and Future	A Halloween History!	Russell Kahn
7	Past, Present, and Future	In Grandma's Kitchen	Mary Harvey
7	Past, Present, and Future	The Glove Family, Part 1	Andrea Cheng
7	Past, Present, and Future	The Glove Family, Part 2	Andrea Cheng
8	Observing the Sky	The Moon	Mary Harvey
8	Observing the Sky	A Star's Story	Rachel Young
8	Observing the Sky	Sun, Moon, and Wind Go Out for Dinner	Sherine Gilmour
8	Observing the Sky	Man in the Moon Mystery Solved	Russell Kahn
8	Observing the Sky	Night Hike	Ariella Tievsky
9	We Use Goods and Services	Real Jobs! Apple Farmer	Abigail Mieko Vargus
9	We Use Goods and Services	No More, No Less, Part 1	Marci Stillerman
9	We Use Goods and Services	No More, No Less, Part 2	Marci Stillerman
9	We Use Goods and Services	Market Day	Sydney Salter Husseman
9	We Use Goods and Services	Traders	Mary Harvey
10	Exploring Sound and Light	Lightning	Jennifer Jesseph
10	Exploring Sound and Light	Signing, Not Singing!	Stephanie Santana
10	Exploring Sound and Light	The Objiwa jingle dress	Clinton Elliott
10	Exploring Sound and Light	The Sweetest Melody	Lydia Nearing
10	Exploring Sound and Light	Firefly Dance	Lindsay Koch

Lexile®	Text Type	Genre	CCSS-ELA	HSS	NGSS
690L	Literary	Realistic Fiction	RL.1.1, RL.1.7, RI.1.1, RI.1.4, RI.1.7, SL.1.1, SL.1.2, L.1.4		K-2-ETS1-1, K-2-ETS1-2
750L	Informational	Social Studies	RL.1.1, RL.1.7, RI.1.1, RI.1.4, RI.1.7, SL.1.1, SL.1.2, L.1.4	1.1.2	
NP	Literary	Rhythmic Poetry	RL.1.1, RL.1.7, RI.1.1, RI.1.4, RI.1.7, SL.1.1, SL.1.2, L.1.4	1.1.1	
510L	Informational	Social Studies	RL.1.1, RL.1.7, RI.1.1, RI.1.4, RI.1.7, SL.1.1, SL.1.2, L.1.4	1.6.2	
590L	Literary	Realistic Fiction	RL.1.1, RL.1.7, RI.1.1, RI.1.4, RI.1.7, SL.1.1, SL.1.2, L.1.4	1.6.2	
550L	Literary	Realistic Fiction	RL.1.1, RL.1.7, SL.1.1, SL.1.2, L.1.4		
NP	Literary	Rhythmic Poetry	RL.1.1, RL.1.7, SL.1.1, SL.1.2, L.1.4		
390L	Literary	Fantasy Fiction	RL.1.1, RL.1.7, SL.1.1, SL.1.2, L.1.4		
NP	Literary	Rhythmic Poetry	RL.1.1, RL.1.7, SL.1.1, SL.1.2, L.1.4		
430L	Literary	Fantasy Fiction	RL.1.1, RL.1.7, SL.1.1, SL.1.2, L.1.4		
410L	Literary	Realistic Fiction	RL.1.1, RL.1.3, RL.1.7, RI.1.1, RI.1.2, RI.1.4, RI.1.7, SL.1.1, SL.1.2, L.1.4		1-LS3-1
680L	Informational	Science	RL.1.1, RL.1.3, RL.1.7, RI.1.1, RI.1.2, RI.1.4, RI.1.7, SL.1.1, SL.1.2, L.1.4		1-LS1-2, 1-LS3-1
NP	Literary	Rhythmic Poetry	RL.1.1, RL.1.3, RL.1.7, RI.1.1, RI.1.2, RI.1.4, RI.1.7, SL.1.1, SL.1.2, L.1.4		1-LS3-1
670L	Informational	Science	RL.1.1, RL.1.3, RL.1.7, RI.1.1, RI.1.2, RI.1.4, RI.1.7, SL.1.1, SL.1.2, L.1.4		1-LS1-2, 1-LS3-1
430L	Literary	Legend	RL.1.1, RL.1.3, RL.1.7, RI.1.1, RI.1.2, RI.1.4, RI.1.7, SL.1.1, SL.1.2, L.1.4		
NP	Literary	Rhythmic Poetry	RL.1.1, RL.1.4, RL.1.7, SL.1.1, SL.1.2, L.1.4	1.5.1	
600L	Literary	Realistic Fiction	RL.1.1, RL.1.4, RL.1.7, SL.1.1, SL.1.2, L.1.4		
430L	Literary	Realistic Fiction	RL.1.1, RL.1.4, RL.1.7, SL.1.1, SL.1.2, L.1.4		
NP	Literary	Rhythmic Poetry	RL.1.1, RL.1.4, RL.1.7, SL.1.1, SL.1.2, L.1.4		
340L	Literary	Myth	RL.1.1, RL.1.4, RL.1.7, SL.1.1, SL.1.2, L.1.4	1.4.3	
NP	Literary	Rhythmic Poetry	RL.1.1, RL.1.2, RL.1.3, RL.1.4, RL.1.7, RI.1.1, RI.1.2, RI.1.4, RI.1.7, SL.1.1, SL.1.2, L.1.4		
400L	Informational	Social Studies	RL.1.1, RL.1.2, RL.1.3, RL.1.4, RL.1.7, RI.1.1, RI.1.2, RI.1.4, RI.1.7, SL.1.1, SL.1.2, L.1.4		K-2-ETS1-1
550L	Literary	Realistic Fiction	RL.1.1, RL.1.2, RL.1.3, RL.1.4, RL.1.7, RI.1.1, RI.1.2, RI.1.4, RI.1.7, SL.1.1, SL.1.2, L.1.4		K-2-ETS1-1
630L	Informational	Social Studies	RL.1.1, RL.1.2, RL.1.3, RL.1.4, RL.1.7, RI.1.1, RI.1.2, RI.1.4, RI.1.7, SL.1.1, SL.1.2, L.1.4		K-2-ETS1-1
420L	Literary	Realistic Fiction	RL.1.1, RL.1.2, RL.1.3, RL.1.4, RL.1.7, RI.1.1, RI.1.2, RI.1.4, RI.1.7, SL.1.1, SL.1.2, L.1.4		
450L	Literary	Realistic Fiction	RL.1.1, RL.1.4, RL.1.7, RL.1.9, SL.1.1, SL.1.2, L.1.4	1.4.3	
540L	Literary	Realistic Fiction	RL.1.1, RL.1.4, RL.1.7, RL.1.9, SL.1.1, SL.1.2, L.1.4	1.4.3, 1.5.3	
NP	Literary	Rhythmic Poetry	RL.1.1, RL.1.4, RL.1.7, RL.1.9, SL.1.1, SL.1.2, L.1.4		
440L	Literary	Folktale	RL.1.1, RL.1.4, RL.1.7, RL.1.9, SL.1.1, SL.1.2, L.1.4	1.5.3	
NP	Literary	Rhythmic Poetry	RL.1.1, RL.1.4, RL.1.7, RL.1.9, SL.1.1, SL.1.2, L.1.4		
400L	Informational	Social Studies	RL.1.1, RL.1.4, RL.1.7, RI.1.1, RI.1.2, RI.1.4, RI.1.7, SL.1.2, L.1.4	1.4.3	
540L	Informational	Social Studies	RL.1.1, RL.1.4, RL.1.7, RI.1.1, RI.1.2, RI.1.4, RI.1.7, SL.1.2, L.1.4	1.3.2	
NP	Literary	Rhythmic Poetry	RL.1.1, RL.1.4, RL.1.7, RI.1.1, RI.1.2, RI.1.4, RI.1.7, SL.1.2, L.1.4	1.4.3	
680L	Literary	Realistic Fiction	RL.1.1, RL.1.4, RL.1.7, RI.1.1, RI.1.2, RI.1.4, RI.1.7, SL.1.2, L.1.4	1.4.3, 1.5.3	
700L	Literary	Realistic Fiction	RL.1.1, RL.1.4, RL.1.7, RI.1.1, RI.1.2, RI.1.4, RI.1.7, SL.1.2, L.1.4	1.4.3, 1.5.3	
NP	Literary	Rhythmic Poetry	RL.1.1, RL.1.2, RL.1.3, RI.1.1, RI.1.2, RI.1.3, SL.1.1, SL.1.2		
480L	Literary	Fantasy Fiction	RL.1.1, RL.1.2, RL.1.3, RI.1.1, RI.1.2, RI.1.3, SL.1.1, SL.1.2		1-ESS1-1
400L	Literary	Fairy Tale	RL.1.1, RL.1.2, RL.1.3, RI.1.1, RI.1.2, RI.1.3, SL.1.1, SL.1.2		
620L	Informational	Science	RL.1.1, RL.1.2, RL.1.3, RI.1.1, RI.1.2, RI.1.3, SL.1.1, SL.1.2		1-ESS1-1
370L	Literary	Realistic Fiction	RL.1.1, RL.1.2, RL.1.3, RI.1.1, RI.1.2, RI.1.3, SL.1.1, SL.1.2		1-ESS1-1
650L	Informational	Social Studies	RL.1.1, RL.1.3, RI.1.1, RI.1.3, SL.1.1, SL.1.2, SL.1.4	1.6.2	
780L	Literary	Folktale	RL.1.1, RL.1.3, RI.1.1, RI.1.3, SL.1.1, SL.1.2, SL.1.4	1.6.1	
760L	Literary	Folktale	RL.1.1, RL.1.3, RI.1.1, RI.1.3, SL.1.1, SL.1.2, SL.1.4	1.6.1	
750L	Literary	Folktale	RL.1.1, RL.1.3, RI.1.1, RI.1.3, SL.1.1, SL.1.2, SL.1.4	1.6.1, 1.6.2	
NP	Literary	Rhythmic Poetry	RL.1.1, RL.1.3, RI.1.1, RI.1.3, SL.1.1, SL.1.2, SL.1.4	1.6.1	
NP	Literary	Rhythmic Poetry	RL.1.1, RL.1.2, RL.1.3, RI.1.1, RI.1.2, SL.1.1, SL.1.2		1-PS4-2
650L	Informational	Social Studies	RL.1.1, RL.1.2, RL.1.3, RI.1.1, RI.1.2, SL.1.1, SL.1.2	1.5.1	
450L	Informational/Literary	Social Studies/Myth	RL.1.1, RL.1.2, RL.1.3, RI.1.1, RI.1.2, SL.1.1, SL.1.2	1.5.3	
660L	Literary	Folktale	RL.1.1, RL.1.2, RL.1.3, RI.1.1, RI.1.2, SL.1.1, SL.1.2	1.5.3	
NP	Literary	Rhythmic Poetry	RL.1.1, RL.1.2, RL.1.3, RI.1.1, RI.1.2, SL.1.1, SL.1.2		